**Paul Gordon**

# White law

*Racism in the police,
courts and prisons*

**Pluto Press**

First published in 1983 by Pluto Press Limited
The Works, 105a Torriano Avenue, London NW5 2RX

Copyright © Paul Gordon, 1983

Cover designed by Michael Mayhew
Cover photograph by John Sturrock/Network

Typeset by Wayside Graphics, Clevedon, Avon
Printed in Great Britain by St Edmundsbury Press
Bury St Edmunds, Suffolk IP33 3TU
Bound by William Brendon Ltd, Tiptree, Essex CO5 0HD

British Library Cataloguing in Publication Data
Gordon, Paul
    White law.
    1. Law enforcement — Great Britain — 2. Great
    Britain — Race relations
    I. Title
    362.3        HV8195

ISBN 0-86104-706-0

# Contents

# Acknowledgements

Several people helped to write this book and it would have been poorer but for their involvement. I am particularly grateful to Frances Webber for her critical reading of the chapter on the courts; Francesca Klug for her comments on an early version of the material on the police and for many conversations which helped to clarify the issues; the Runnymede Trust whose library provided most of the material used in this book; and, for much needed musical sustenance, the Durrutti Column, Comsatt Angels and the Blue Nile (and Alisdair Gordon who provided them), Jack Bruce, John Martyn and, especially, Robert Wyatt. At Pluto Press, Richard Kuper encouraged the project through from start to finish and Paul Crane and Fanny Campbell saved me from some literary barbarisms and helped me say what I meant. I owe a particular debt to the Institute of Race Relations whose work over the past decade, more than any other source, has informed the writing of this book.

In the end, the burdens (and some joys) of writing this book were shared with three people. Hilary Arnott, Phil Scraton and Joe Sim each found time from their own important commitments to read the manuscript in its entirety and to discuss my difficulties as they arose. No one could realistically have hoped for such a combination of critics, informants, sub-editors and friends.

# Preface

Many people took comfort from Lord Scarman's remarks in his report on the 1981 Brixton riots that there was no institutionalised racism in Britain. It was a country, he said, which did not as a matter of policy discriminate against black people. Nor were the direction and policies of the Metropolitan Police racist. At worst, he said, public bodies and private individuals might unwittingly discriminate, and some police officers might occasionally manifest racial prejudice on the streets. But there was no institutional racism. Politicians and police alike could relax in the knowledge that this great judge, himself a liberal of course, had exonerated them from such a serious allegation.

This book is not a reply to the Scarman report nor a critique of it, although no one writing about 'race' in Britain in the 1980s can completely ignore Scarman and the proposals he offered the British state. Rather, it is about the notion Scarman so easily swept aside: institutional racism and the harsh reality that flowed from it in the 1970s and 1980s in a key area of state policy and practice – the criminal justice system.

This system, comprising the police, the courts and the prisons, is important because, as the coercive arm of the state, it is used increasingly as a means of social and political control. It is important too because there is a tendency to see the state as consisting only of the police. They are considered problematic while the rest of the system is ignored.

The criminal justice system is not the only source of oppression of black people. There are many aspects of state control (or attempts at control) of the black population which are not dealt with here. This is not because they are unimportant. Some – for example, schooling, youth work and the welfare state – have been dealt with elsewhere by others much better qualified to do so.[1] Other aspects require detailed exposition in their own right. This seems particularly true of an area touched on early in this book, that of the administration of race relations, what has been called the 'race relations industry', especially in the light of the new 'Scarman generation' of race experts, representatives and spokespeople in research institutes, local government and the media.[2]

In order to understand the criminal justice system and its racist practices, it is necessary to situate it in its overall context. Chapter 1 looks at how racism came to be institutionalised in Britain in the early 1960s through the definition of black people as a problem to be controlled, both by keeping them out through immigration control, and by the social management of those already here through anti-discrimination laws and the race relations industry. That definition has dominated British thinking about race ever since, and has determined the attitudes and policies of state agencies towards black people.

Nowhere has this been more cruelly evident than in the case of the police. Chapter 2 shows that complaints of racist police behaviour are old as the modern black presence in Britain. It shows that such complaints cannot be shrugged off as unfounded or explained away by reference to a few prejudiced individuals, but that there is a pattern and a consistency in the now considerable volume of evidence available. Chapter 3 looks at the other side of policing the black community: the development of 'community relations' work, moves to recruit black people into the police and the strategy of co-option of blacks into policing and mediating their mistrust and hostility. Chapter 4 looks at the extent of individual racism within the police but suggests that this in itself cannot explain police racism. It goes on to examine what institutional racism actually means in policing.

The police are not, however, the only state agency in conflict with black people. Indeed, encounters with the police are frequently only the beginning of a series of encounters with the criminal justice system. Chapter 5 examines the criminal courts in relation to black people, the charges used, the procedures invoked, and the sentencing, behaviour and attitudes of judges and magistrates.

The ultimate expression of law, George Jackson once said, is 'not order – it's prison'. Increasing numbers of black people are being sent to prison and the black prison population is much higher than one would expect, given the size of the black population. Chapter 6 looks at the evidence of racism in prison, at the treatment of black prisoners, at prison staff's support of fascist ideas, and at the position of people in prison as a result of immigration law.

The approach in these six chapters is largely descriptive. The final chapter tries to make sense of the evidence, to understand why this state of affairs has developed and to locate it in its broader context of the long drawn out political and economic crisis that has been the state of British society for over a decade.

The purpose of this book is to aid the process of understanding racism, particularly with regard to the police, the courts and the prisons, and of grasping its central importance to the struggle for social, economic and political freedom.

# 1. State racism

It was alleged by some of those who made representations to me that Britain is an institutionally racist society. If by that is meant that it is a society which knowingly, as a matter of policy, discriminates against black people, I reject the allegation.
Lord Scarman, *The Scarman Report*, 1981[1]

**Immigration control: defining 'the problem'**

British racism, as the ideology of the superiority of white over black, justified centuries of physical conquest and subjugation of half the world's countries. It justified, too, the plunder, genocide and rape that accompanied it. But when the sun set on the British empire, it did not set on racism. Rather, racism came home, to continue to serve as justification for exploitation.

In the years immediately after the second world war, there were severe labour shortages in Britain. Refugees from European countries were allowed to stay on in the country as European Voluntary Workers, often working in the most appalling conditions and subject to severe restrictions. They had to work in whatever jobs the Ministry of Labour prescribed for them and some (for example, Ukrainian prisoners of war) were liable to be thrown out of the country if they were unable to work. Paul Foot cites the case of a boy who lost his sight through an accident at work. He was deported to Germany.[2]

Despite the availability of such a pool of cheap and easily disposable labour as the European refugees and displaced persons, the demands of the British labour market were still not satisfied. The imperial past, however, had ensured that there was another source of such workers. The British Nationality Act of 1948 laid down that citizens of Commonwealth countries were British subjects, entitled to enter Britain, to work here and, though nobody appeared to consider it likely at the time, to settle permanently. In the 1950s, organisations such as London Transport, the British Hotels and Restaurants Association and the Ministry of Health all recruited labour in the Caribbean islands. Throughout this period the extent of immigration into Britain closely matched the level of vacancies in the British labour market. By the late 1950s, however, the demand for labour was declining and government discussions, which had begun as early as 1951, about the control of black immigration, resumed. They were given added impetus, not only by an increasingly vocal racist lobby, but also by the perceived social costs of immigration. Social costs included not just the price of housing, education, health care and social service provision, but also the threat of social disruption, such as occurred in the anti-black riots of 1958 in Nottingham and Notting Hill.

It was to such issues that the Commonwealth Immigrants Act of 1962 addressed itself. The Act applied to Commonwealth citizens and to holders of United Kingdom passports which had not been issued either in the UK or by a High Commission abroad. It therefore distinguished between British citizens who would be predominantly white, and those whose passports had been issued in a colony and would be mainly black. The racism of the law went further. All those who were made subject to immigration control had now to obtain a Ministry of Labour voucher before they were allowed into the UK. Category A vouchers were issued to those with a specific job. Category B vouchers were issued to those with a recognised skill or qualification in short supply in Britain. Category C vouchers were issued to all others. Not surprisingly, given the history of colonial exploitation and underdevelopment of the Caribbean and the Indian sub-continent, most of the people from these areas would be eligible only for Category C vouchers.

It is at this point that the process of the institutionalisation of racism begins. Here racism is no longer simply a disparate ideology, but is accepted officially and enshrined in the law. The 1962 Act and the 1965 Labour government White Paper, *Immigration from the Commonwealth*,[3] (which abolished Category C vouchers altogether and reduced the number of other vouchers) defined the problem as the presence of black people in Britain, and not as the response of white society to that presence. The answer to the problem was therefore obvious. It was to control the numbers of black people – the fewer the numbers the smaller the problem, and the better for race relations. This was the official logic: it was responsible for the early controls and has dominated all thinking about race since. What it meant in practice was spelled out by Robert Moore in his book *Racism and Black Resistance in Britain*:

> The argument about numbers is unwinnable because however many you decide upon there will always be someone to campaign for less and others for whom one is too many. Since you have admitted that black people are a problem in themselves, it is impossible to resist the argument for less of them. Even if new migrants are reduced to nil, the argument can be shifted to the numbers of dependants; when they are reduced it can be shifted to the question of illegal immigrants; when these are shown to be few in number it can be argued that the government is cooking the books. In the last analysis if you play the numbers game then black people already here and every black child born here is a problem and the discussion shifts to questions of deportation.[4]

This is exactly how the debate about immigration has developed in the past two decades. Such legal niceties as citizenship with a right of entry and abode in the UK could be dealt with as expediency demanded. In 1968 thousands of Asians in East Africa, who had kept their citizenship of the United Kingdom and Colonies rather than adopt the citizenship of the newly independent states, were threatened with expulsion and began to arrive in the UK. The Labour government simply passed a law stipulating that only those with a 'close connection' with the UK were free from immigration control. This 'close connection' was that of birth in the UK, descent from a UK-born parent or grandparent, or naturalisation or registration in the UK as a citizen. In other words, it was defined so as to exclude black UK passport holders and to include white. Labour's Commonwealth Immigrants Act, passed in Human Rights Year, was later held by the European Commission on Human Rights to be racially discriminatory, and also an interference with the right to family life and degrading treatment.[5]

This somewhat *ad hoc* approach to the control of black immigration was fully systematised by the Immigration Act of 1971. The Act divided people into patrials and non-patrials. The former were citizens of the UK and Colonies, born in the UK or with UK-born parents or grandparents; they were free from immigration control and could enter and settle in the UK. Other UK and Colonies citizens who had been settled in the UK and been ordinarily resident for five years also became patrial. All others, generally speaking, were non-patrials. They had no right of entry into the UK and no right of abode.

The 1971 Act marked the end of black immigration for settlement and indicated the end of the process begun in 1962. It changed the status of the immigrant from that of settler to that of migrant worker who may enter the country to do a specific job for a specific period but once here has no right of settlement and few other rights. Thus, the British state ensured that it would continue to have access to cheap labour should the need arise, but it could do so without social costs. It only remained to deal with the anomalies of a citizenship system which did not match that of immigration – and that was eventually done by the British Nationality Act of 1981. Patrials were given British citizenship and only they have the right of entry and abode in the UK. A lesser citizenship, carrying no right of entry to the UK and few other rights, was given to all those who were not patrial.

In less than 20 years the position of the black citizens of the UK and Colonies underwent a radical transformation to meet the demands of the British economy and British politics. At each stage – in 1962, 1965, 1968, 1971, 1981 – racism has been advocated by government and opposition alike (even when they differed in detail). It has been sanctioned – and institutionalised – in the fabric of British society.

British immigration controls have always involved internal as well as external controls. The former operated to get rid of people already in the country, while the latter were designed to keep people out in the first place. The Aliens Act of 1905 gave the Home Secretary power to deport 'undesirable aliens', especially those who were unable to support themselves and their families and who were therefore costing the state money. (In this can be seen the precursor to modern restrictions on immigrants having 'recourse to public funds'.) But the power of expulsion was quite narrow and could be exercised only following conviction for an offence and a recommendation for deportation by the court. Alternatively, the court could certify that within 12 months of arrival the alien was destitute or was wanted for an extraditable crime. He or she was then liable to deportation.

The first world war and its attendant xenophobia brought controls on aliens of a more far-reaching nature. The Aliens Restriction Act 1914 was passed on the first day of war and gave the Home Secretary virtually unlimited powers to exclude and deport aliens. The powers were not withdrawn after the war. They were extended for one year by the Aliens Restriction (Amendment) Act 1919 and renewed annually thereafter until 1971. To the court's power of recommending deportation following conviction was added a power for the Home Secretary on his own initiative to deport those whose presence he considered not 'conducive to the public good'. These powers applied only to aliens. Commonwealth citizens were immune from deportation.

The Commonwealth Immigrants Act 1962 introduced the first controls on the entry of people from the Commonwealth; it also implemented the first controls on those who were here already and those who would be allowed entry in the future. For the first time, the Home Secretary had power to deport Commonwealth citizens, although this was not so extensive a power as in the case of aliens. There was no power to deport those whose departure was thought 'conducive to the public good' but only those who had been convicted and recommended for deportation by the court. In addition, a Commonwealth citizen ordinarily resident in the UK for five years acquired immunity from deportation.

Those who were subject to control and were refused entry but entered nevertheless could be removed from the country, but only if apprehended within 24 hours of arrival. A Commonwealth citizen was under no obligation to appear for examination by immigration officers and evasion of control altogether was not an offence.

But increasingly the law began to close in. By its nature the extent of evasion of control could not be measured. The Labour government's White Paper of 1965 implied that it was extensive and stated an intention to crack down on illegal entrants. The Commonwealth Immigrants Act 1968 placed a *duty* on all Commonwealth immigrants to pass through immigration control. A person who did not and who was apprehended within 28 days could be removed without appearing before a court, and evasion of control also became a criminal offence. The Immigration Appeals Act of 1969 extended the power of deportation and allowed the Home Secretary on his own initiative to deport any immigrant who broke a condition attached to entry.

The screw of internal controls turned further with the Immigration Act of 1971. The immunity from deportation enjoyed by Commonwealth citizens living here for five years was restricted to Commonwealth citizens who were ordinarily resident when the Act came into force. Anyone arriving after that was liable to deportation until they became a British citizen. Commonwealth citizens also became liable to deportation on the grounds that their presence was not 'conducive to the public good'. In each case, the wife and children of a deportee could also be deported. Those deemed to be illegal entrants could be removed by order of the Home Secretary at any time and the previous time limits on removal were abandoned. Appeal against removal as an illegal entrant became possibly only *after* removal.

The courts, prodded by cases taken by the Home Office, seemed only too eager to extend the scope of immigration control to people already living here. The courts have ruled that an illegal entrant is not simply someone who avoids immigration control altogether, as was commonly understood when the new Immigration Bill was being debated. The term now includes those who deceive immigration officers, even where the deception is made unwittingly. For example, the Court of Appeal ruled in 1977 that a false passport produced by an entrant's husband made her entry illegal, even though she was illiterate.[6] Similarly, large numbers of people who came to the UK on work permits have been held to be illegal entrants because they did not disclose the existence of dependent children or because false references were supplied to obtain work permits. It has not mattered that in many cases the deception was practised not by the permit holders themselves but by employment agencies.

The courts further extended the definition of 'illegal entrant' in the case of *Zamir* in 1980. The House of Lords ruled that it was not just a question of telling the truth and not deceiving immigration officers. Immigrants had a positive duty to tell the immigration officer about anything that might be material, whether or not they were questioned about it. In other words, immigrants had to be mind-readers or else run the risk that they would be deemed later to have entered illegally because they did not say something now considered to be important. Although this decision was reversed by the House of Lords in the case of *Khera* in February 1983, the general drift of the law was not stopped. These issues are dealt with in greater detail in chapter 5.

There had to be some form of machinery to enforce these internal controls, to carry out surveillance of those liable to deportation and to find those suspected of being illegal entrants. The police had been involved in the control of immigration at least since the first Aliens Act; the Special Branch in particular had been responsible for the surveillance of the many political refugees who had come to Britain from Russia and Eastern Europe. The police, together with the immigration service, continued this function in relation to Commonwealth immigrants. The next chapter shows that this has had far-reaching consequences for relations between the police and black people.

The police and the immigration service were not the only agencies enforcing Britain's internal controls. As attention has turned away from external controls to controls operating inside Britain and to questions of supposed illegal immigration, so increasingly have other agencies – social security officers, housing departments, hospitals – taken it on themselves to question black people about their immigration status and their entitlement to state benefits. In 1974 it was reported that the education department in the London Borough of Ealing had been asking the parents of black children to produce their passports before they were taken on the school register.[7] In 1976 it was reported that 185 Asian women attending the Leicester General Hospital's ante-natal clinics had been asked to produce their passports. One woman who refused was denied care even though she had previously had a baby at the hospital.[8]

Such action has received tacit, and sometimes explicit, encouragement of government. In 1979, for example, the Department of Health and Social Security advised hospital administrators that they 'had a part to play in ensuring that the principles of eligibility are adhered to' and that they should watch out for those who were not 'ordinarily resident' and therefore not entitled to free treatment. The circular was called, with characteristic British state tact, 'Gatecrashers'. In the same year, the Department of the Environment was advising the Association of Metropolitan Authorities that requesting to see a passport in housing cases might be 'a reasonable means of clarifying points'. Also housing authorities suspecting a breach of immigration controls 'would no doubt wish to consider whether they should draw it to the attention' of the Home Office. Similarly, social security regulations introduced in 1980 created for the first time a distinction between those lawfully settled in Britain. Previously, all those without enough to maintain a minimum standard of living were entitled to state benefits. The 1980 regulations changed this. Now benefits can be refused to people here without permission or here on the condition that they do not receive 'public funds'. They may also be refused to people who have been sponsored to come to Britain (usually dependants of people settled here); the sponsor is held liable to maintain the sponsored person. This distinction resulted in the interrogation of more and more black claimants by social security staff on the grounds that they may not be entitled to claim.

Immigration control operates on two levels. It keeps black people out of the country altogether. And it operates against people who are already here on the grounds that they may be here unlawfully or that they may be seeking some benefit to which they are not entitled. Since it is not possible to tell a 'legal' immigrant from an 'illegal' one, or an immigrant from a citizen, the answer is to suspect all who appear to be immigrants.

## Managing 'the problem': anti-discrimination and integration

Immigration control defined black people as a problem for the state, hence their numbers had to be controlled. But it was not the only response to the presence of black people in Britain. It might keep the numbers down, but there was still the question of those who were already here and who, short of enforced removal, were here to stay. There was, in other words, a problem which had to be managed. Attempts began in 1962 when the Commonwealth Immigrants Advisory Council was set up to advise the Home Secretary on matters relating to the welfare of immigrants. Labour's White Paper of 1965 saw this management of race relations begin in earnest.

The White Paper attempted to give substance to the bones of the argument that immigration control was unnecessary for good race relations. Immigration control was to be drawn even tighter, but life would be improved for black people here. The crux of the matter was put in Roy Hattersley's self-serving aphorism of the time: 'Without integration, limitation is inexcusable; without limitation, integration is impossible.' Within months of the White Paper the Race Relations Act 1965 was passed. This statute prohibited discrimination only in places of public resort, leaving untouched extensive discrimination elsewhere, and enacted a half-hearted prohibition against incitement to racial hatred, a provision which very quickly proved unworkable. A Race Relations Board was established to enforce the Act, supported by a network of local conciliation committees.

A report published in 1967 by Political and Economic Planning (written by, among others, Geoffrey Howe QC) claimed that discrimination persisted, varying from the 'massive to the substantial'.[9] In 1968, the year of the Commonwealth Immigrants Act, Labour passed another Race Relations Act. This time, the law was intended to deal with employment; housing; the provision of goods, facilities and services to the public; and discriminatory advertisements. The Race Relations Board was given increased powers to investigate complaints but was almost entirely reliant on conciliation and the courts to enforce the law. But then, as Sivanandan succinctly puts it, the law 'was not an act but an attitude'.[10]

A key part of this education was the creation of a new state-funded Community Relations Commission, replacing the old National Committee for Commonwealth Immigrants – a 'nation-alisation' of a key sector of the rapidly expanding race relations industry. The Commission and its network of local community relations councils were charged with the task of promoting good community relations and of advising government and other bodies.

It was obvious that the 1968 Act would scarcely dent the surface of racism in Britain. It was equally obvious that discrimination could have been dealt with had the desire and political will to do so existed. The reality, however, was otherwise. Government had institutionalised racism and made it respectable in immigration control; it had also discovered that there were votes to be won (and lost) on the question of 'race'. This was brought home to Labour and Tory alike when, in 1964, a Labour cabinet minister lost his seat to a Tory, one of whose slogans ran, 'If you want a nigger for a neighbour, vote Labour.' Labour promptly abandoned its previous opposition to immigration control.

At the same time, no government could afford the social costs of uncontrolled racism. The racist riots of 1958 remained in the minds of politicians, but perhaps more threatening to social order was the development of a large and marginalised section of the working class, excluded from society purely on grounds of colour. The point was candidly expressed in the 1969 report of the mammoth Survey of Race Relations:

> Finally, the concentration of coloured immigrants in certain sections of employment and their absence in others coupled with the fact that there has been little or no change between 1961 and 1966 gives most cause for concern. If this pattern continues into the 1970s then the assessment that the situation is still fluid and has not hardened into a *class-colour or colour-caste structure* may well be over-optimistic.[11] (emphasis added)

The contradiction in state policy therefore remained. Racism was used to keep black people out, but it was socially costly and dangerous. It would only be a matter of time before further changes were required.

The government White Paper, *Racial Discrimination*,[12] published in 1975, expressed continuing concerns. It said, 'It is no longer necessary to recite the immense danger, material as well as moral, which ensues when a minority loses faith in the capacity of social institutions to be impartial and fair.' The evidence was all around. Political and Economic Planning had shown in 1974 that while discrimination against black people with qualifications had declined, unskilled workers would meet discrimination in between one-third and one-half of all applications for jobs.[13] In 1975, the Runnymede Trust pointed to extensive discrimination in the allocation of houses by the Greater London Council.[14] In 1976 the Metropolitan Police were complaining to the parliamentary Select Committee on Race Relations and Immigration of the tendency of black youths to combine against the police to attempt to rescue arrested friends. In the same year, police and black people fought a pitched battle on the streets of Notting Hill at the end of the Carnival (see chapter 2).

The writing was clearly on the wall and the point had not been lost on the authors of the White Paper. 'It is vital', they wrote, 'to our well-being as a society to tap these reservoirs of resilience, initiative and vigour in the racial minority groups and not allow them to lie unused or to be deflected into negative protest on account of arbitrary and unfair discriminatory practices.' The resulting Race Relations Act of 1976 owed much more to such sentiments than to any humanitarian concerns for the well-being of black people.

The 1976 Act extended the scope of the law to cover also indirect discrimination, that is, where practices are not intentionally discriminatory but discriminate in their effects. It made very limited provision for 'positive action' to promote equality of opportunity, and it provided for aggrieved individuals to take their cases direct to industrial tribunals (in employment cases) and to the courts. The Community Relations Commission and the Race Relations Board were merged in the new Commission for Racial Equality, which was given considerable powers to conduct investigations into possible discrimination and to assist individual complaints. In addition, the law against incitement to racial hatred was strengthened.

Despite such changes, the law has not succeeded in ending discrimination. Only a tiny minority of cases alleging discrimination in employment actually succeed and even then damages awarded are generally derisory. There have been few cases of discrimination in other areas which have gone to the courts, and the CRE has been largely ineffective in its formal investigations. The law on incitement to racial hatred has been used rarely, with little impact, and most racist material has gone unchallenged.[15]

The law has not succeeded, therefore, in the tasks envisaged for it by the 1975 White Paper. Consequently, after the 1981 riots, a new round of heart-searching and head-scratching began. In a critical report issued in 1981, the parliamentary Home Affairs Committee (successor to the Select Committee on Race Relations and Immigration) lambasted the CRE, which is supposed to enforce the Act, for its 'incoherence'.[16] The Committee, including both Labour and Tory MPs, made no explicit reference to the summer's events, but the stridency and uncompromising tone of its criticisms stemmed from a belief that the CRE had failed precisely where it most needed to succeed. In the words of the 1975 White Paper, it had failed to prevent the 'resilience, initiative and vigour in the racial minority groups . . . to be deflected into negative protest'. It had failed to prevent the anger and frustration of black people, especially black youth, spilling over onto the streets. Lord Scarman suggested in his report that 'if alienation among the black community is not to develop, there should be a more ready recognition of the special problems and needs of the ethnic minorities than hitherto.'[17]

The reasons for the failure of the law and of the CRE are many, and are certainly more complex than mere 'incoherence'. Even in its own terms, the government made a major blunder right at the start by appointing to the CRE chair a former Tory minister responsible for immigration. The appointment might well have been intended to show employers and administrators that they had nothing to fear, but it was hardly designed to win black people

over to the CRE cause. In addition, the government had exempt-
ed itself from the scope of the Race Relations Act 1976 by provid-
ing that anything done under statutory authority was not covered
by the law. It therefore contested in court the right of the CRE to
investigate the administration of immigration control. The
government also considerably delayed approving the Commission's draft code of practice on the elimination of discrimination at
the workplace. In the private sector, the CRE was obstructed by
the ingrained racism of employers and, in some cases, of trade
unions when it attempted to carry out formal investigations of
individual companies. In industrial tribunals the Commission has a
good record of representing complainants but few people have
chosen to fight their cases this way and the majority of applications
have, in any case, been unsuccessful. In the four years of the law to
mid-June 1981, there were just over 1200 applications to tribunals.
Over half did not proceed to a hearing, and of those which did,
only 102 were upheld while 492 cases were dismissed. Just over 8
per cent of all cases therefore succeeded in obtaining a tribunal
decision. The successful complainants received little by way of
compensation. Only one was awarded £1000 for the discrimination suffered; most received less than £200.

Where the law succeeded, however, was in the creation of a
black managerial middle class – managerial, that is, in the sense
of management of the 'black problem'. Thus, Sivanandan wrote
of the situation on the eve of the 1976 Act that:

> the Commission took up the black cause and killed it. With the
> help of its 'black' staff and its 'black' experts, with the help of
> an old colonial elite and through the creation of a new one, it
> financed, assisted and helped to set up black self-help groups,
> youth clubs, supplementary schools, cultural centres, homes
> and hostels. It defined and ordained black studies; it investi-
> gated black curricula; it gave a name and habitation to black
> rhetoric . . . It has taught the white power structure to accept
> the blacks and it has taught the blacks to accept the white
> power structure. It has successfully taken politics out of the
> black struggle and returned it to rhetoric and nationalism on
> the one hand and to the state on the other.[18]

This process continued with the Commission for Racial Equality and the local community relations councils. At a national and local level, respectively, they gave the appearance of 'something being done' but they acted to co-opt black militancy and black demands and grievances. They spoke on behalf of black people and made autonomous black organisation all the more difficult. They nationalised the black struggle – or at least they tried to. For like 'race relations' laws generally, race relations organisations stood in a conflicting and contradictory position. On the one hand, they needed to win the confidence and support of black people. On the other, they had to be acceptable to the white establishment. The contradiction has persisted and is a hallmark of community relations work. Community relations councils that try to address themselves to the real issues facing their local black population frequently run into trouble and accusations of 'extremism' and of being 'unrepresentative'. Exactly these criticisms have been levelled at the Commission for Racial Equality itself whenever it has attempted to speak out on such matters of concern to black people as government legislation on nationality or immigration. In his enquiry into the Brixton disturbances, Lord Scarman noted that he had received a number of such criticisms. CRCs, he said, had to recognise that their 'primary duty' was to 'foster harmony, not to undermine it'. Scarman concluded that it was time the role of CRCs was reviewed. The question raised, of course, is who defines what 'fostering harmony' means? And whose harmony is being fostered?

More important than all this, however, is the basic contradiction in state policy towards black people. That is, you cannot consistently and openly discriminate in immigration control, and at the same time argue that discrimination is wrong. As an employer once asked at a conference: 'Why is it wrong for me to refuse to have any of these people in my firm when the government is refusing to have them come into the country. If the government doesn't want them, why should I want them?'[19] Any educational function the law might have was weakened from the start. While the contradiction might be dealt with so long as there was money to buy off the discontent of black people, sooner or later the contradiction would sharpen and become more apparent. The Race Relations Act was passed as the British economic crisis deepened. Pumping money into black areas and black projects was simply not on the agenda, at least not on the scale required. The CRE was faced with the situation in which the race relations law became irrelevant to the majority of black people as it was unable to protect them from permanent unemployment, from the rigours of immigration laws, or from the ravages of the police.

# 2. Police against black people

Nobody has done more in this country for race relations than the police.
Jim Jardine, chair of the Police Federation, 21 March 1979[1]

## Communities under attack

Joe Hunte was one of the many West Indians who had come to Britain after the war in search of a job and a decent living. He was also one of the first people to document police abuse of black people. The title of his pamphlet, *Nigger Hunting in England?*, derived from statements allegedly made by police officers leaving their stations saying they were going 'nigger hunting'. The pamphlet was published in 1966 by the London Region of the West Indian Standing Conference, and identified a number of issues and cited numerous cases. These included racist abuse of black people by the police, a failure to protect black people, a suspicion among the police that black people were engaged in criminal activity, and police harassment of the social life of black people by raiding allegedly illegal drinking clubs. Hunte's report identified the very issues which would be at the heart of policing and black people until the 1980s.

Hunte's pamphlet looked specifically at the London Borough of Lambeth where the author had lived for many years. The problem of racist policing has persisted but is not unique to Lambeth, as we shall see. Major police operations against black people have been launched on several occasions in the Brixton district of Lambeth. In 1975, the activities of the Special Patrol Group (SPG) in the area led directly to the formation of the

Lambeth Campaign Against Police Repression which demanded their withdrawal from the area. SPG tactics followed a pattern which had been established elsewhere – road blocks, early morning raids on people's homes and random and aggressive stop and search operations. In 1978, 120 officers, more than half the total SPG strength, were brought into the area because of the supposed 'high crime' rate. Over a thousand people were stopped and 430 arrested. Forty per cent of the latter were black, although black people were only 20 per cent of the population in the area. Those arrested by the SPG included ten young blacks who were arrested in their dinner hour near Stockwell Manor School and charged with 'sus', the offence of being a suspected person loitering with intent to commit an offence. (The use of this law is dealt with in more detail below.)

Such operations and tactics brought relations between the police and the people in the area, especially black people, to such a low ebb that, in an unprecedented move, the local council resolved in March 1979 to set up an independent enquiry into police/community relations. The previous month, three workers at the Council for Community Relations in Lambeth (CCRL) were arrested in a police raid on their offices. The raid followed a stabbing in Clapham and police were looking for someone believed to be wearing a sheepskin coat. Police knew that one of the CCRL workers owned such a coat and went to the office to make an arrest. Two other workers there, also black, told police that they too had sheepskin coats. They too were arrested. All three were later released without charge and the CCRL withdrew from the local Police Liaison Scheme in protest.

The Lambeth enquiry received 275 submissions, amounting to 1500 pages of evidence, from individuals and organisations in the borough. The submissions included a large number of general and specific allegations of police misconduct including intimidation, arbitrary arrest, misuse of police powers, harassment, and failure to observe Judges' Rules, which are supposed to govern the treatment and questioning of suspects in police custody. (One black clergyman had asked the police what advice they expected him and others to give to young blacks and was told, 'Get them off the streets.')[2] The report of the enquiry, which was finally published in January 1981, concluded that 'the condition of community/police relations in Lambeth is extremely grave'.[3] The *New Statesman* commented that the report indicated that 'A leading aim of policing in Lambeth – and in other areas with large black communities – appears to be to lay siege to the black population.' The police, who had been invited to co-operate, declined 'with regret' to submit evidence.

The warnings of the Lambeth enquiry were ignored completely. Even while the working party sat in late 1979 and summer 1980, the Special Patrol Group was again deployed in the borough. But the biggest police operation, and one which was to have dramatic consequences, was yet to come. On Monday, 6 April 1981, Operation Swamp '81 was launched; its function, as described in the written instructions to police officers was:

> to flood identified areas on 'L' District to detect and arrest burglars and robbers. The essence of the exercise is therefore to ensure that all officers remain on the streets and success will depend on a concentrated effort of 'stops', based on powers of surveillance and suspicion proceeded [sic] by persistent and astute questioning.[4]

In the six days of Swamp '81, 943 people were stopped and 118 arrested. Just over half of those stopped were black and over two-thirds were under 21. Although 75 charges followed, only 22 related to burglary or theft. Swamp '81 failed to apprehend large numbers of offenders; more importantly it brought bad feeling between the police and black people in the area to a pitch. On Friday, 10 April, police were stoned by angry youths and on Saturday, 11 April, even as Swamp continued, Brixton burned.

This was not, however the end of the matter. Whilst Lord Scarman's enquiry sat during July 1981, 176 police armed with crowbars and sledge hammers raided 11 homes and business premises, supposedly in search of petrol bombs. None was found. Windows were smashed, floorboards were ripped up and doors broken down. The raid was described by local MP John Fraser as 'overreaction and provocation'; to the local community, it looked like an act of revenge. Assistant Commissioner Dear, who was asked to report, thought that the damage was 'unavoidable', while William Whitelaw, the Home Secretary, said he would not question the judgement of the police.[5]

Lambeth, however, is but one area which has been subject to racist policing. A similar history could be written of other areas throughout Britain, including those where rioting occurred in the summer of 1981. In Merseyside, Margaret Simey, chair of the Merseyside Police Authority and a critic of policing methods in the area, had warned as long ago as 1971 that:

> The coloured community is fed up with being hounded. No one is safe on the streets after 10 p.m. One gang we know has given the police an ultimatum to lay off within two weeks or they fight back. It could lead to civil war in the city.[6]

The parliamentary Select Committee on Race Relations and Immigration enquiry into police/immigrant relations in 1971–72 had been told in Liverpool of extensive police use of racist terms, frequent allegations of threatened and actual assault and denial of rights on arrest. A decade later, the Merseyside Area Profile Group, presenting evidence to the Select Committee's successor, the Home Affairs Committee, surveyed the literature on police relations with black people on Merseyside through the 1970s. The evidence, it said, pointed to the

> dangerously poor relationship between the black community and the various arms of the law . . . In Liverpool, relationships between the police and the black community are frequently tense, with widespread accusations of police maltreatment and victimisation by the courts.

The Group concluded that the major patterns of police racism outlined to the Select Committee in 1971–72 were still valid. Within 18 months, Liverpool too was burning.

In Birmingham, Gus John's report for the Runnymede Trust, *Race in the Inner City*, published in 1970, described relations between the police and black people in Handsworth as suffering from a 'massive breakdown'. The Thornhill Road police station, he said, was one of the buildings most dreaded and hated by black people in Handsworth. John himself said that it was certainly not dramatic to describe the relationship between police and black men in Handsworth as 'one of warfare – and anything but cold'. Such tension, the author pointed out, was the result of police suspicion that almost all black people were involved in crime, the use of stop and search powers, and the racist attitudes of police officers. One police officer told John:

> When these people have their heads full of pot and alcohol, spurred on by the thumping beat of these reggae records, they are not humans any more, and only those who don't like themselves would set out to treat them as humans.[7]

Almost ten years after John had carried out his research in Handsworth, the organisation All Faiths for One Race (AFFOR) published a collection of interviews with young black people and their parents in the area. It showed that little had changed. The accounts offered highlighted the complaints of previous studies – racial abuse, harassment, assault and a feeling that the police were beyond any legal or community control. Over one-third of those interviewed recounted at least one incident of harassment or brutality they had experienced themselves, while nearly every other person interviewed knew of an incident involving a close friend. Some could see what was likely to happen if things did not change:

> If the police are going to be continually harassing people, black people, then there is going to come a stage where they are not going to accept it. They are going to stand up for themselves, they are going to fight back.[8]

In Southall, in the late 1960s and early 1970s, the black residents were quickly shown police indifference to racist attacks when police did nothing to apprehend those who attacked shops and premises and did nothing when, in 1970, a gang of skinheads rampaged through the town. By 1973, allegations of police misconduct were so numerous that the Indian Workers' Associaton, the Pakistani Action Committee and Afro-Caribbean Association asked the Home Secretary to set up an independent enquiry into police brutality. No such enquiry was forthcoming.[9] At the same time, however, the local community relations council had commissioned Dr Stanislaus Pullé to examine complaints against the police. Applying a rigorous test of selection, Pullé analysed and further investigated 50 cases where black people in Ealing had made formal complaints against the police. Pullé's report, *Police/immigrant relations in Ealing*, was published by the Runnymede Trust in November 1973 and concluded that there was a '*prima facie* case against the police on charges of brutality and partial conduct against the immigrant community in Ealing'. Although it said nothing radically new, the Pullé report aroused a storm of protest from the Metropolitan Police. The Commissioner, Sir Robert Mark, attempted to dissuade the Runnymede trustees from publishing the report and, when they declined his 'offer' detecting a note of duress, he issued a statement attacking the document. Later, in his autobiography, Mark accused the Runnymede Trust of publishing a report 'which they knew to contain inaccuracies, to be misleading and quite certain to provoke racial disharmony'.[10] This unprecedented police response (coupled with reports that the police in Southall tried to find out who had given evidence to Pullé) can perhaps be explained by Pullé's thoroughness (he rejected the complaints of those known to be 'anti-police') and by its publication by an organisation generally respected by the establishment.

When some six years later in April 1979, the police cordoned off Southall on the occasion of a provocative National Front meeting there, thus creating what they revealingly called a 'sterile zone' in the town centre, they did so in order 'to teach Southall a lesson' for the past. In a police action without precedent in Britain, 2756 police officers, including units of the Special Patrol Group, occupied the area. In the ensuing confrontation, the police killed one man – Blair Peach – fractured the skull of another, caused innumerable injuries to hundreds, arrested 700 people and charged 342. Demands for an official public enquiry made by the Commission for Racial Equality, the TUC and the Anti-Nazi League, among others, came to nothing. No police officer was ever prosecuted for Blair Peach's death even though the inquest jury, in returning a verdict of 'death by misadventure', accepted that he had been killed by the police. Eleven eye witnesses told the inquest under oath that Peach had been hit by a police officer; there was no evidence that he had resisted arrest, assaulted police, or even tried to flee. The Unofficial Committee of Enquiry set up by the National Council for Civil Liberties came to the 'inescapable conclusion' that Peach had been killed by a blow deliberately inflicted by a member of either Unit 1 or Unit 3 of the Metropolitan Police Special Patrol Group.[11]

A report on the day's events by Southall Rights concluded that police behaviour had

> left a deep scar on the people of Southall that will take years to heal. The racial abuse that accompanied the violence, the wanton destruction of property . . . and the pursuit of persons running away and/or trying to seek shelter, all give the lie to any suggestion that the Police were merely defending themselves, and are consistent with Superintendent Hurd's comment early in the afternoon that Southall needed to be 'taught some discipline'.[12]

Lambeth, Liverpool, Handsworth and Southall: four different areas. But similar descriptions could be written of others.

In Archway, north London, in early March 1981, six police cars and a helicopter responded to a reported incident at Archway School. Police arrived to see a boy on a moped, which they immediately suspected was stolen and rushed to arrest him. In fact, the bike was not stolen. Pupils at the school alleged the police assaulted black pupils and called them 'black bastards'; one white girl was told, 'Listen you fucking nigger-lover, I'll have you.'[13] The police stated that such allegations were 'the usual standard sort of propaganda about police going in with big boots on the kids. We did not go in with big boots. We responded as we should have responded . . . The response was excellent.'[14]

In Hackney, east London, in 1981 several car- and van-loads of police and dogs responded to a report of a robbery in Chatsworth Market. They indiscriminately arrested black youths and detained them for 12 to 18 hours. In contravention of the Judges' Rules, their parents were not informed. Only one person was subsequently charged – with possession of cannabis.[15]

In Moss Side, Manchester, in March 1981, police followed a black youth carrying a two-foot length of bamboo into a library and arrested him for carrying an offensive weapon. A crowd gathered and soon 16 police vehicles and 28 officers were on the scene. The Manchester Black Parents' Association declared that Moss Side police station 'has long been regarded by the black community as the operational base of a racist army of occupation'.[16]

In North Kensington, west London, 100 police officers raided a hostel for black youths in July 1981. They ran through the building breaking down doors but no arrests were made. Nor was any explanation forthcoming.[17]

In April 1982, violence in the Notting Hill area erupted as 100 police officers in riot gear were brought in after a crowd had freed two people arrested by the police. Their behaviour in clearing the streets was described by an eyewitness local councillor as 'organised police vandalism'. The Home Secretary told parliament it was 'an example of what is needed'.[18]

In Stoke Newington, north London, the police unlawfully entered the home of an elderly black couple, David and Lucille White, in September 1976. The couple were badly injured by the police and later falsely charged with assaulting the police. They were acquitted and in an action for damages were awarded £51,000 for what the judge described as 'a catalogue of violence and inhuman treatment'. The police, he added, in trying to cover up their wrongful acts, had been guilty of 'monstrous, wicked and shameful conduct in the name of justice'.[19]

These are no isolated, localised aberrations, but reflect a national picture. When in 1971 the parliamentary Select Committee took evidence on police/immigrant relations, it was warned by the Natinal Council for Civil Liberties that 'the worsening situation between the police and the black community is very serious indeed.' The Institute of Race Relations concluded its submission that the Select Committee would have wasted its time if it failed to recognise that 'Police/black relations are deteriorating fast to the point where violent solutions will soon be sought.'

By the end of the 1970s the Institute, with some feeling of *déjà vu*, was warning the Royal Commission on Criminal Procedure that if Britain was moving towards 'two societies, one black, one white – separate, unequal' (the words of the US National Advisory Commission on Civil Disorders), then 'the police will have had no small part to play in that polarisation.'[20]

This is the general picture of policing and black people in Britain. Such policing has involved biased use of the law against black people, over-policing of black meeting places and events, appalling treatment in police stations, failure to deal properly with complaints and failure to protect black people from racist violence and harassment. Each of these is considered in turn.

## Street harassment

One of the complaints which emerges consistently from accounts of policing and black people is that the police do not enforce the law impartially, and that particular laws are used against black people, especially section 4 of the Vagrancy Act 1824, the sus law, and what the Institute of Race Relations described as 'sus 2', the enforcement of the immigration laws against people living in Britain. In addition, there have been complaints about the police use of their stop and search powers and their powers of arrest.

Concern within the black community about 'sus' – the offence of being a suspected person loitering with intent to commit a criminal offence – has existed for a long time. In 1978 Clare Demuth's report, published by the Runnymede Trust, showed statistically what black people had known all along: that black people were disproportionately arrested for sus. Thus, in 1976, in the Metropolitan Police area 2112 people were arrested for sus. Of these, 887 – 42 per cent – were black, yet in 1975 (the last year for which figures were then available) only 12 per cent of those arrested in the area were black and only 11 per cent of those arrested for offences of theft and dishonest handling were black. According to the police, what this meant was simply that greater numbers of black people were involved in street crime. According to black people and those involved with civil liberties work, however, the police used sus to keep black youths off the street and constructed evidence after arrest. Young black people would be deterred by the presence of a large number of police offiders and the threat of arrest, and would be encouraged to stay out of the area altogether.[21] But sus, in its targeting of black youths, was also an important part of the process by which the police criminalised black people – that is, used the law against them so as to show them as criminals.

Eventually, after a lengthy struggle by the Scrap Sus Campaign (an organisation based in the black community) coupled with demands for repeal of the law by organisations such as the Institute of Race Relations, the National Council for Civil Liberties, the Catholic Commission for Racial Justice and the Runnymede Trust, sus was repealed. The victory was an important one, but the Criminal Attempts Act 1981, which repealed sus, also created *new* criminal offences of interfering with a motor vehicle and attempt. To many, the new law meant the replacement of sus, not its end.

Sus, as many of its opponents had argued, was not used throughout the country, but only in certain areas, notably the Metropolitan Police area. In Liverpool, for example, there was no apparent bias in the use of sus, but there was bias in the use of stop and search powers. This had been highlighted by the Merseyside Area Profile Group in its evidence to the Home Affairs Committee in 1980. The following year Ann Brogden reported preliminary findings of her research into stop and search. This showed increasing friction between police and youths over the use of stop and search, increased use of the power, and a widespread belief that the police discriminated against black youth.[22] Such beliefs were reflected in the report of the Merseyside Police Authority, published in the wake of the 1981 riots. The report on relations between the police and the public concluded that the 'sheer weight of adverse comment alone compels us to recognise that a gulf exists between the police and certain sections of the community in Liverpool 8.' Most frequently alleged in such adverse comment was harassment by the police through the use of their stop-and-search powers and the manner in which such powers were used.[23]

The use of stop and search to harass black people on Merseyside was nothing new. Dorothy Kuya, herself a Liverpool-born black, recalls how in the 1950s her father, a very 'quiet and gentle old man', was frequently stopped and searched as he walked home in the middle of the night from his shift on the docks.[24]

Nor is such harassment confined to Liverpool. A study in Notting Hill showed that black men were four times more likely to be stopped in the street by police than white men, and a black man was 30 times as likely to be stopped as a white man in circumstances which he perceived as harassment.[25]

The Institute of Race Relations' pamphlet, *Police Against Black People*,[26] had cited a number of cases of arbitrary arrest and arrest where unnecessary violence had been used. Occasionally, even the courts would uphold a case against the police for such arrests. Thus, in 1970 Roger Daly was awarded over £3000 for false imprisonment, assault and malicious prosecution by the police[27] and in 1981 Trevor Rhone was awarded £673 against two sergeants for unlawful arrest and malicious prosecution in 1977. The police were also ordered to pay costs. Rhone, a 43-year-old black man, had been accosted by the police when walking home from a party in north London. They had stopped him saying, 'What are you doing out at this time of night, Sambo?'[28]

Research by the Home Office itself, however, has provided the most conclusive evidence of bias in arrests. Philip Stevens and Carole Willis, in *Race, Crime and Arrests*,[29] have shown that in the case of assault the arrest rate per 100,000 population was 77 for white people. But for Asians it was 124 and for Afro-Caribbeans it was 466. In the case of robbery, the figures were 18, 13 and 160 respectively. The researchers declined to come to any conclusion, but did say that the arrest rates for black people were so much higher than might have been expected that one had to ask whether they accurately reflected involvement in crime. If they did not, then it was possible that some of the difference could be accounted for by the fact that the suspicions of police officers bore disproportionately on black people. This conclusion is borne out not just by the researchers' own findings that black people were 14 or 15 times more likely to be arrested than white people for sus and 'other violent thefts', but also by further research by Maureen Cain and Susan Sadigh some years later. Cain and Sadigh found that West Indians were much more likely to be charged with victimless crimes than were white people, that is, they were charged as a result of police initiative rather than as the result of any action by any victim. The offences included motoring, sus and drunkenness. Thus, while just over 30 per cent of whites arrested were charged with this kind of offence, the figure for black arrests was over 46 per cent. However, when drinking and driving offences (for which there is usually some objective evidence) were excluded, the difference was even more startling: just under 19 per cent for whites but over 46 per cent for blacks. In addition, over 46 per cent of the West Indians arrested were under 21, compared to only 12 per cent of white people arrested. The evidence, the researchers concluded, 'is therefore entirely consistent with the view that young blacks are indeed disproportionately harassed.'[30]

## Passport raids and checks

If black people are more likely to be arrested in certain circumstances and especially more likely to be stopped and searched on the street, then they were even more likely to be stopped, searched, questioned and detained under the provisions of the Immigration Act 1971.[31] It is clear that the control of immigration also involved controls operating *within* Britain. The 1971 Act gave the police and immigration service considerable powers to detain and question those they believed might be illegal entrants or in some other way in breach of immigration law. Even before the Act came into force in January 1973, the Metropolitan Police had created an Illegal Immigration Intelligence Unit at Scotland Yard, the purpose of which was to 'receive, collate, evaluate and disseminate information relating to known or *suspected* offenders' (emphasis added). In the first year of its operation, the Unit carried out some 219 enquiries concerning alleged illegal entrants and made 73 arrests.

These enquiries included several major 'passport raids' – operations at workplaces and homes in search of people in breach of immigration law. The first major operation took place in October 1973. Over 13 separate addresses in north and east London were visited by police and immigration officers. A number of people were taken to police stations, including one man who had lived in Britain for six years. Despite protests, the Home Secretary, Robert Carr, rejected demands for an enquiry into the raids and a further raid took place later the same month. Then, a rooming house for Asian men in north London was raided by police early one morning. The men alleged that the police showed no warrants and abused the residents. One man who was unable to produce his passport – because he had sent it to the Home Office – but who could produce the Home Office official receipt and his employment voucher, was nevertheless taken to the police station and held for several hours before local police confirmed that they had checked his immigration status in 1970 and found it to be in order.

Further raids took place in 1975 and 1976, and in December 1977 there was a major raid on Bangladeshi houses and restaurants in Newcastle-upon-Tyne. Sixty-two people were questioned and 24 detained. Of these, 18 were released the next day, but six were further detained in Durham Prison. Three of these were subsequently deported, but the others, including one man who was held in prison for six weeks, were released.

The Home Office claims that no central records of passport raids are kept, but between the first raid in October 1973 and April 1978, a few months after the Newcastle raids, police and immigration officers had carried out at least 25 major operations of this kind. The largest raids were, however, still to come.

In May 1980, the Bestways Cash and Carry Warehouse and other Bestways premises in London were raided by 45 police and immigration officers. Thirty-seven people were arrested as illegal entrants, including some who had produced their passports when taken to their homes by the police. One man who had lived in the UK for 22 years was detained for seven hours. None of those detained was allowed to see solicitors. The home of one man was searched without his permission and without a warrant and left in a ransacked state. Those arrested were given an opportunity to collect and produce documents showing the legality of their presence only *after* they had been taken to a police station. In one case, police made no attempt to verify the details given by a man who quoted the number of the certificate granting him citizenship of the UK.

Less than two weeks later, 76 police and immigration officers questioned over a hundred workers at the Hilton Hotel in Park

Lane, London. Four of those arrested were detained for several hours before satisfying police that they had a right to be in Britain.

One month later, on 20 June, more than a hundred police and immigration officers raided the Main Gas factory in north London. Although the information on which the raid was based related to West Indian workers, all black workers at the factory were questioned. Forty-seven people were questioned and 31 arrested.

When parliament was debating the Immigration Bill in 1971, government ministers were keen to quash any ideas that the new law could or would be used as the basis for a witch-hunt of the black community. Yet, it is hard to see the passport raids as anything but this. Despite repeated assurances from ministers that there were no random raids, such operations have continued. Even the review of procedures, announced by the Home Secretary in 1980 following the widespread condemnation of the raids that year, did little to change things. The review restated that the police and immigration service had a right to carry out raids and demand to see passports. Not surprisingly, given the experience of previous government 'assurances', the review was soon to be followed by further raids.

In February 1981, 12 Bengali restaurant workers in north London were woken by police and immigration officers and told to produce their passports. No arrests were made. In response to protests, the government this time argued that the procedures introduced as the result of the review did not apply. The review related to 'major operations' but not to 'routine enquiries'. The February raid was of the latter kind and was not therefore covered.

Passport raids are not, however, the only way in which the black community is harassed under the Immigration Act. Police officers also have power to stop and question people suspected of being in breach of law. For example, a Nigerian was arrested when he went to a police station to offer bail for a friend; a Nigerian refugee was asked for his passport when stopped for a minor road traffic offence, and a Ghanaian who reported a burglary at his home was asked for his passport.

Although such harassment can happen to anyone who appears in any way be 'foreign', the brunt of such harassment falls on the black community. In an unprecedented move after the 1980 raids the general secretaries of the Transport and General Workers' Union and the General and Municipal Workers' Union warned that such raids were 'producing a situation more reminiscent of the apartheid situation in South Africa than in Britain'. The Joint Council for the Welfare of Immigrants (JCWI) submitted to the Royal Commission on Criminal Procedure that the police role in immigration control was a 'major source of suspicion and mistrust' with which many black people viewed the police, and the Institute of Race Relations, which described the Immigration Act provisions as 'sus 2', stated its belief that:

> these provisions make every black person in this country a potential suspect in the eyes of the police, and the harassment and suffering they create for many people is not justified by the number of 'real' illegal immigrants detained . . . these provisions help create an attitude towards black people which is incompatible with the police's function of protecting all sections of the community.[32]

The Royal Commission decided not to consider police powers under immigration law, even though both the JCWI and the Institute of Race Relations had established that police methods were doing harm to relations between the police and black people. Discussion of the issues was therefore excluded from the Commission's report.

### Social and political life

Police harassment of black people in places known as social and political centres has occurred at least since the end of the second world war. In an article published in *Pan-Africa* in 1947,[33] Mary Winters and J. Hatch of the Tyneside Inter-Racial League described the police campaign against cafes owned by black people on Tyneside. This included attempting to have their food licences revoked, setting watch on certain cafes with police officers standing outside the doors and windows peering in to try to detect anything that might be used against the owners, asking customers for their identity cards and searches and questioning. In addition, the police brought charges against two cafe owners for allowing prostitutes to assemble on their premises. The convictions of these two men were overturned on appeal and costs awarded against the police. The police then resorted to use of the war-time Defence Regulations, which gave them extensive powers, and three cafes were closed. Police harassment of the two acquitted cafe owners resulted in one going back to India and the other giving up his business. The whole experience, in the words of one local solicitor, left the black community feeling 'victimised and hounded out'.

Police harassment of black social locations was one of the complaints documented by Joe Hunte in his report on Lambeth, cited earlier in this chapter. In Notting Hill, police attention has focused on the Mangrove restaurant for over a decade. The Mangrove, begun in the late 1960s by Frank Critchlow, quickly established itself as a restaurant and unofficial advice centre for black people in Notting Hill. It was first raided in February 1969 by police looking for drugs. None was found and there were no arrests. Another raid took place in June 1969, and although again no drugs were found, Frank Critchlow was shortly afterwards to lose his licence. In May 1970 Critchlow was charged with serving food after 11 p.m. and in August several hundred people marched in protest at police harassment of the Mangrove and those who frequented it. Nineteen people were arrested after fighting when police tried to dictate the route of the march. (The trial of the 'Mangrove Nine' is dealt with in chapter 5.) Between 1972 and 1977, the police visited the Mangrove an estimated 40 times, usually in search of people 'wanted by the police'. In July 1977, the restaurant was raided by 50 police and Frank Critchlow and five customers were arrested. Critchlow was charged with allowing his premises to be used for consumption of an illegal drug, an offence for which he would have lost his licence and, presumably, the restaurant. The others were charged with other drug offences. But in June 1979, Critchlow and two defendants were acquitted and only three charges of simple possession were upheld.[34]

The Mangrove's problems were not over. On Christmas Eve 1981, the restaurant was again raided, this time by 50 members of the Metropolitan Police Immediate Response Unit, a specially trained squad equipped with riot shields and flame proof overalls (in this case not carrying any marks of identification). The area round the Mangrove was sealed off, but only one arrest was made from the raid itself.[35]

Other black social centres have had the same treatment, even if for shorter periods. In January 1981, for example, the Holloway Night Cafe in north London was raided by the Special Patrol Grop and Desmond Riley, who runs the cafe, and his brother were arrested for obstruction. Two weeks previously a meeting had taken place at the cafe, attended by the police community liaison officer and the chief executive of the borough, to discuss relations between the police and black people in the area. Neither the community liaison officer nor the superintendent in charge of the Holloway area had been consulted or informed of the SPG raid.[36]

The Institute of Race Relations in *Police Against Black People* documented a number of cases of police raids on black youth clubs. These included a raid by the SPG on the Metro youth club in Notting Hill in May 1971 on the pretext that a youth wanted by the police had entered the premises. Unnecessary violence was used by the police and 16 black youths were arrested. None was convicted of any offence. In October 1974, police raided the Carib youth club in Cricklewood, north west London. Over a hundred police with dogs and riot shields took part and roads were sealed off. All of those arrested were eventually acquitted. Indeed, during the trial the judge told the jury, 'You may feel that there can be no question of mistake. Either Sweeney [a member of the club management committee] committed the offence, or the police officers concerned have made the whole thing up.' None of those arrested was convicted.[37]

Not only black meeting places are liable to be harassed by the police. As the Institute of Race Relations has shown, excessive numbers of police at events with special significance for black people is also an aspect of harassment. Nowhere has this been more evident than the policing of the Notting Hill Carnival over the years. Until 1976, the Carnival had attracted large numbers of people and been peaceful. Then the police attempted to have the Carnival banned and, when this failed, mobilised 1500 officers for the occasion. It was, as the Carnival Development Committee said in a statement, 'an insult . . . an unnecessary army of policemen which instilled fear in the revellers'. There were serious disturbances for the first time in the Carnival's ten-year history. The Metropolitan Police Commissioner, Sir Robert Mark, was unrepentant about police tactics. He told the press that 'no go areas' in the capital would not be permitted. Crime, he said, 'is not negotiable as far as we are concerned. If there is a crime we will decide how to deal with it.'[38] In his report for 1976, Mark listed the Carnival in the section on 'Public Order' and commented that 'the incidence of crime in the vicinity . . . fully justified the decision to deploy officers in such strength.'

Carnival in 1977 was again regarded as a 'Public Order' affair by the police; indeed in the Commissioner's report it was listed under 'Demonstrations'. This time some 6000 police were deployed over the two-day event. In 1978 the number of police had risen again to 9000 and by 1981 Carnival was involving 13,000 police officers.

In Leeds bonfire night has an importance for the local black community similar to that of the Notting Hill Carnival. In 1975, a show of strength from the police provoked a riot among those present, the police having ignored a previous agreement that they would maintain a low profile. When the cases arising from the event came to court, there were 21 acquittals out of 24 charges. (The trial is dealt with in more detail in chapter 5.)

One of the reasons the police persistently harass the Mangrove is that it is known as a place frequented by black radicals. The law on drugs provided a justification for such raids. The demonstration against police harassment of the club in August 1970 ended in disorder because police attempted to dictate to the demonstrators the route they should take. The police were quick to blame 'outside agitators' for the trouble, although ten of the 19 people arrested had addresses in North Kensington, and Home Secretary Reginald Maudling was reported to have demanded a police report on the local black community. The *Guardian* reported that he would have 'a complete dossier within 48 hours. The Special Branch has had the movement under observation for more than a year. Police now regard Black Power as, at least, worthy of extremely tight surveillance.'[39]

The policing of black politics has taken more dramatic and drastic forms. The police action at Southall in April 1979 was not just a gross denial of the right of a community to demonstrate against its political opponents, but was also in line with stated police intentions of teaching Southall 'some discipline'. Similarly, when 15,000 people marched on the Black People's Day of Action in March 1981 in protest at police handling of the New Cross fire, in which 13 young black people lost their lives, violence was provoked by a police presence of 3000 officers, and also a police decision to alter the agreed route of the march without consulting the march organisers. The march was angry but predominantly peaceful and without incident, but was subsequently portrayed by the popular press as the 'Day the Blacks Ran Riot in London'.[40]

**Police custody**

Racist policing is not confined to the streets but continues in police treatment after arrest. Simha Landau, an academic on sabbatical at the Home Office Research Unit, examined all police decisions concerning juveniles in five divisions of the Metropolitan Police in late 1978. In all, he looked at 1708 decisions. In relation to crimes of violence, burglary and 'public disorder and other offences', and especially in relation to the last two, black juveniles were treated more severely by the police than white juveniles, being more likely to be charged immediately than referred to the juvenile bureau where they would only receive a warning. The most important and likely explanation for this difference was the existence of 'situational factors', that is, the interaction between the juveniles arrested and the police. It was argued that false police perceptions of black youths as being more aggressive and antagonistic than white youths could affect police decisions to prosecute.[41]

Black people in police custody also appear more likely to 'confess' to offences. John Baldwin and Michael McConville of

Birmingham University showed that in London 60 per cent of black defendants confessed, compared with 49 per cent of white defendants. In Birmingham, a similar picture emerged, with respective figures of 58 per cent and 47 per cent. Only one-fifth of all West Indian defendants went into court without having made or having attributed to them a confession or other damaging statement.[42]

Not all such 'confessions' are fabricated by the police or extracted under duress, but clearly some are. Satnam Kane, for example, worked in a petrol station in Southall. He was charged with the theft of £50 and after interrogation by the police admitted guilt. His boss subsequently rang the police to say that a mistake had been made and the money was accounted for. The Director of Public Prosecutions said later that there was insufficient evidence to prosecute the police officers involved.[43] Similarly, in July 1977, Sharon Banks was arrested for theft of £50 from a supermarket. Under Judges' Rules Sharon, who was only 17, should have been questioned only in the presence of a parent. She was denied access to them and eventually 'confessed' to the theft. The money was later accounted for.[44]

Fortunately neither Satnam Kane nor Sharon Banks ended up in prison as a result of police malpractice. George Lindo was not so lucky. He spent nearly two years in prison after he had signed a 'confession' to having stolen £67 from a betting shop. When he signed the statement he had been in police custody for 15 hours and later, in the presence of his solicitor, he repudiated it. He was, nevertheless, convicted and sentenced to two years' imprisonment. One of the officers involved in the case, who later admitted to the forging of statements in the search for the 'Yorkshire Ripper', was suspended and resigned in September 1978. Although the Director of Public Prosecutions and the Registrar of Criminal Appeals were informed, George Lindo's solicitor was not advised of this crucial development. It was only in June 1979 that Lindo's conviction was crushed on appeal. Lindo had been released pending the appeal in March. Two weeks later, he would have been eligible for release on parole. In 1982 he was finally awarded £24,000 in compensation.[45]

More recently, Errol Madden, an 18-year-old black art student, was stopped and searched in the street by police. They found two model cars which he had bought but was unable to remember where. He was taken to Battersea police station, threatened by police officers and told that he should confess to the theft of the model cars. Eventually, after having been locked up for two hours, a statement of 'confession' was dictated by the police and Madden signed it. He was charged and remanded. Errol Madden was later able to produce the receipt for one of the cars, which had in fact been on him at the time of his arrest, and a witness came forward to support his purchase of the second car. The charges to which Errol Madden had 'confessed' were then dropped. No action was ever taken against any of the officers involved, even though the Police Complaints Board commented that Errol Madden had been 'subjected to some distinctly un-professional behaviour' and that the episode 'reflects very badly on the Metropolitan Police'. The officers involved were simply to be given 'strict advice' by senior officers.[46] Such failure of the complaints system will be looked at in more detail later in this chapter.

Virtually unrecognised in the recent discussions about deaths in police custody has been that over the years a significant number of black people have died while in police custody.[47] In 1971 Aseta Sims died in Stoke Newington police station in London. A police doctor found deep bruising and swelling in the head, but could not determine the cause of death. Police maintained that she had been drunk. The inquest verdict was death by misadven-ture, but there was no conclusive evidence of alcohol poisoning or anything similar. In 1974, Stephen Bernard, who had a history of mental illness, was taken to a police station instead of to hospital after his relatives had phoned for an ambulance. Al-though he had had a 'seizure' he was held at the police station and eventually charged with damaging police property. In court he was given a discharge and recommended for admission to hospi-tal. He died the following morning. The same year, John Lamalette died only days after his wife had seen him being held by police officers and punched on both sides of the neck. He died of a blood clot resulting from having had an artery constricted. In 1977, a Mauritian nurse died in police custody within one hour of being pronounced by a police doctor as fit to be detained. In 1979, Swarm Singh Grewal was found dead in his cell at Southall police station two-and-a-half hours after his arrest. Police claimed that he died from inhalation of his own vomit, but requests by his wife and family to see the body were refused and they were allowed to see it only days later at Hammersmith Hospital. There they remarked on the heavy bruising to the head, arms and leg.[48]

Exactly what happened in these and other cases of black people dying in custody we shall never know. We do know, however, that Winston Rose, who died in July 1981 after a struggle with police, was unlawfully killed, according to the inquest verdict. Rose, who was in custody under the Mental Health Act, died in a police van on his way to a mental hospital. Although he had a history of mental illness, he had no history of violence, according to the coroner. Yet 12 police officers were involved in his apprehension, some apparently having gone to the scene believing they were looking for an escaped criminal, others believing Rose was violent. Once again, the Director of Public Prosecutions declined to prosecute any of the police officers involved on the grounds that there was 'insufficient evidence'.[49]

## Police complaints

The system for making complaints against the police has worked even less well for black people than it has for whites. Joe Hunte in his 1966 pamphlet described the complaints system as inadequate and unsatisfactory. The following year the Campaign Against Racial Discrimination (CARD) *Report on Racial Discrimination* noted that 'Complaints of brutality or ill-treatment by the police occur with disturbing frequency. They are invariably denied.' Two years later, in 1969, the mammoth 'Rose Report' on British race relations, *Colour and Citizenship*,[50] attached the greatest importance in its discussion of the police to reform of the police complaints system.

Rose's recommendation was supported by John Lambert, author of *Crime, the Police and Race Relations* which, like *Colour and Citizenship*, had emerged from the Institute of Race Relations survey of British race relations. Lambert, in a talk given at the Institute in 1970, warned, however, that without support from the police any change in the system was bound to fail.

In 1972, the Select Committee on Race Relations and Immigration, reporting on relations between the police and black people, concluded that the main contentious issue was the way in which complaints were handled. The Committee therefore recommended to the Home Secretary that he 'take urgent steps to introduce a lay element into enquiries into complaints against the police'. The generally complacent tone of the Select Committee report was flatly contradicted by Derek Humphry's *Police Power and Black People* published in the same year.[51] On complaints Humphry wrote:

> To continue to argue the case for reform of the system whereby members of the public may lay complaints against policemen is to risk boring the reader. The futility of complaining has been demonstrated frequently in earlier chapters and thousands of words have been written by others of the hypocrisy of the police being their own investigators and judges.

While the Home Secretary pondered the Select Committee's recommendation, Stanislaus Pullé's report on complaints in Ealing showed quite clearly just how great was the difference between the theory of the police complaints system and its actual practice. Such pressure, combined with publicity about extensive corruption in the Metropolitan Police, forced the government to introduce the Police Act 1976. A new Police Complaints Board was established to oversee the investigation of complaints which remained in the hands of the police.

This minor reform did little, if anything, to stem the ebb of public confidence in the complaints system. That it could achieve little was shown by a number of cases, some involving black complainants. In 1977, for example, a Nigerian student was assaulted so badly by the police that he had to have one testicle removed. Charges brought against him for being drunk in charge of a vehicle were dismissed. No police officer was charged or disciplined. Indeed, none seemed even to have been properly questioned by investigating officers and the Director of Public Prosecutions accepted without question a dossier saying that the guilty officers could not be found. The Nigerian was eventually awarded £1500 by the Criminal Injuries Compensation Board and given £4000 and £1000 costs by the Metropolitan Police if he would drop his claim for damages. According to the *Observer*, the two officers responsible and the superintendent who was supposed to investigate the complaint were all subsequently promoted.[52]

Errol Madden, another black person, also failed, as we have seen, to achieve any satisfaction from the police complaints system, even though the Police Complaints Board itself accepted that he had been subject to 'some distinctly unprofessional behaviour'. The only person who faced disciplinary charges was the station sergeant, for 'failing to keep good order in the charge room'. The two officers who actually charged Madden were simply given 'strict advice' by a senior officer. The Metropolitan Police refused to give an undertaking that Madden's statement of complaint – material which would not have been available to them in the usual course of civil litigation – would not be used in preparing the police defence in the action for false imprisonment and malicious prosecution which Madden also pursued. The police therefore not only investigated themselves, but also used the evidence obtained through the complaints system itself to defend themselves against civil action, the only other means of recourse open to the complainer.

At the end of 1982, the High Court ruled that the Police Complaints Board had made a mistake in refusing to consider the cases of both Madden and Trevor Rhone. The Board had said that it could not investigate their cases because the Director of Public Prosecutions had declined to prosecute. For it to do so would place the police officers involved in 'double jeopardy', something the complaints system was supposed to avoid. The court said that double jeopardy was best understood as meaning 'no man should be tried twice for the same offence' and the word to be emphasised was 'tried'. The Board had put a 'different and erroneous' interpretation on the phrase; it should not regard itself as bound by the DPP's decision and ought therefore to investigate the complaints.[53]

More damning evidence has come from the Home Office itself. In a report published in 1982 (only after details had been leaked in *The Times*) Philip Stevens and Carole Willis showed that very few complaints by black people succeeded. Complaints by black people were likely to be of assault, the complainants were more likely to have been under arrest, to have been reported for an offence, or to have a known criminal record. These factors alone, the researchers concluded, would lead one to expect a low substantiation rate for complaints made by black people. This low rate of success was also, however, due to the generally low substantiation rates for complaints of assault and for complaints made by people who are themselves arrested. Both of these complaints made up a substantial proportion of complaints by black people. In relation to complaints of assault the Police Complaints Board itself had said in 1980 that 'the investigating officer is perhaps more likely to be influenced by early experience of his own and to be more ready to accept the policeman's account of what took place than that of the complainant.' In other words, it concluded, lack of evidence was not the sole reason for low substantiation rates: 'investigations into alleged assault are not perhaps always as thorough as investigations into less serious complaints.'[54]

Lord Scarman, in his report on the Brixton riots, added his weight to the argument for reform because of the 'considerable evidence' he had received of the 'lack of confidence in the impartiality and fairness of the procedure, not only among members of the ethnic minority communities but generally'. Shortly afterwards, the Home Affairs Committee launched an enquiry on the subject, but stopped short, yet again, of recommending that the whole system be made completely independent of the police.

### Racial violence and self-defence

The police have failed to protect the black community against racist violence and harassment. There is nothing new about racial violence in Britain, nor anything new in police failure to protect black people from such attacks. Concerted attacks against black people in Britain took place as early as 1919 in London, Bristol, Cardiff and Liverpool. In Cardiff, white youths climbed on to the roofs of black people's homes and threw slates and bottles at them. In Liverpool, white people rioted for several days, beating up black people and smashing their homes. One man who tried to fight back, Charles Wootton, was pursued to the docks where he drowned trying to escape from his attackers. Although such attacks were initiated by white people, the vast majority of those arrested were black. In a similar vein the response of the government was not to deal with those who perpetrated the violence, but to encourage the victims to 'go home' by offering them cheap passages on ships.[55]

In the years after the second world war, black people were again the subject of concerted attacks. Such violence reached its peak in the rioting against black people in Nottingham and Notting Hill in 1958. Less than a year later, a West Indian carpenter, Kelso Cochrane, was stabbed to death in Notting Hill. His killer was never found. It was, as Sivanandan reminds us, 'to prove the first of many such failures' by the police. Joe Hunte, in *Nigger Hunting in England*, criticised the police for failing to protect black people, and in 1970 Victoria Randall, carrying out research in Leamington Spa for the Runnymede Trust,[56] noted that the most tense period for relations between the police and the black community had been during 1964–66 when there was a series of racist attacks and harassment, including the smashing of windows and the burning of crosses. The attitude of the police, then as now, was to play down the incidents as the work of 'outside' hooligans, rather than of racists, and for the most part they failed to supply sufficient officers to provide adequate protection. The situation changed only when some black people began buying guns to protect themselves. The police then started to provide the necessary protection.

In 1968, the Pakistani Workers' Union complained of police failure to protect Asian workers going home from work in London's West End. In 1970 a wave of 'Paki-bashing' broke out in the East End of London. In three months 150 people were seriously assaulted in the area, and in April Tosir Ali, a 50-year-old kitchen porter, was stabbed to death only yards from his home in Bow. The Pakistani Workers' Union demanded an enquiry into the failure of the police to act, while a Scotland Yard statement denied there was any evidence to suggest that black people were attacked any more than whites.[57] The Pakistani Students' Federation estimated that one-quarter of its members had been attacked and similar stories emerged from Southall and Wolverhampton.

In 1971, nine people were injured when a petrol bomb was thrown into a party in Sydenham, south London,[58] an attack which was to have a tragic parallel almost a decade later, when 13 young people lost their lives in a fire at a party in nearby New Cross. In 1973, the Unity Centre, a black bookshop and meeting place in Brixton, was the object of an arson attack and the *Sunday Times* reported that it was the eleventh such attack in the area in a six-week period.[59] Stanislaus Pullé's report of the same year on police complaints described police handling of one case of harassment – a case containing the full range of complaints that have been made of police handling of racial violence. The original police response to the harassment of an Asian man by a group of white youths, which included smashing his windows on ten occasions, was inaction and a refusal to arrest the culprits, even after they had been identified. When the man then resorted to methods of self-protection, the investigating inspector threatened to arrest him for possession of an offensive weapon. The police suggested that the motive for the harassment lay in an argument the man had had with some delivery boys over the purchase of furniture.[60]

In 1975, Ronald Jones, a black bus conductor, was fatally injured after a row with a passenger over a fare for a dog. In the same year, Hector Smith, a West Indian, was shot dead in Glasgow by Brian Hosie, a member of the National Front. Hosie was alleged to have told police, 'Niggers mean nothing to me. It was like killing a dog. Niggers make good fertilisers.'[61] The same year, Labour MP Paul Rose began compiling a dossier of right-wing violence and claimed knowledge of a thousand incidents in a 12-month period.[62]

Racial violence, however, reached a new height in 1976. In that year, Enoch Powell returned to the subject of race after a relative silence of some years. Powell seized on a government error in immigration figures, and his accusations of a government cover-up were eagerly seized on by most of the press. At the same time, the press prominently reported 'revelations' that a homeless family, expelled from Malawi, was being housed in a four-star hotel – 'Scandal of £600-a-Week Immigrants', as the *Sun* headlined its front page on 4 May. In the wake of such reporting racial violence quickly followed, as shown by a statement issued by the Institute of Race Relations on which the following account is based.

On 2 May the *News of the World* reported: 'One slips in on every boat'. Three days later Asian parents in Redbridge made an appeal for the safety of their children after they were repeatedly assaulted on the school playground. On 6 May, the *Sun* headlines read: 'Another 20,000 Asians are on the way' and 'Storm over two-wife immigrant'. That night an Asian shop in west Essex was attacked several times. Next day, the *Sun* reported, '4 Star Asians run up £4,000 bill' and 'Queue jumping rumpus'. The *Guardian* on 9 May headlined 'Asians rile neighbours' (though the report was in fact about how Malawians were set upon by white families at the reception centre for Malawi refugees). The next day a concrete slab was hurled through the window of a Hackney Asian's house and paraffin poured over furniture, which was then set alight. Four days later a 40-year-old Bengali in Oldham was beaten and knifed by a gang of 15 white youths, and shopkeepers and restaurant owners told of repeated attacks. On 17 May the *Daily Express* wrote of 'Asian flood warning' and two days later a West Indian mother in Poplar asked for help against constant attacks, threats on her children, obscene letters and paint daubing on her house. That night two students, one Indian and one Jordanian, were stabbed to death in Woodford, three miles away. That same morning the *Guardian* had reported 'Migrant figures kept covered'; on 25 May the *Daily Mirror* wrote 'Another Race War warning by Enoch'; the *Daily Express*, 'Immigrant Racket Row'. A week later a pregnant West Indian was kicked by police on the street in Brixton, and three days later an Asian youth was stabbed to death by a gang in Southall.

The murders – of the two students Dinesh Choudbury and Ribhi Al-Haddida, and of Gurdip Singh Chaggar in Southall – were not the only killings of black people during 1976. They were followed by Emmanuel Alombah, who was shot dead by a complete stranger in west London, and Mohan Gautam, a 76-year-old Asian woman who was tied to a chair and burned to death in Leamington Spa in August. Police denied that there was any racial motive in the latter killing even though the woman had been able to tell police just before she died that her attackers were white and despite a background of fascist activity and racial violence in the area.

The same year also saw a delegation to the Prime Minister from the Standing Conference of Pakistani Organisations and the Asian Action Group calling for an enquiry into racial violence and the activities of right-wing groups. *The Times* reported that the Prime Minister assured the delegation that the government and the police were 'determined to take every possible measure to protect the minority communities from violence and intimidation'. The police, he said, 'fully understood the seriousness of the situation'. He was sure they behaved with responsibility and awareness.[63]

In 1977 Bethnal Green and Stepney Trades Council launched its enquiry into racial violence in London's East End. The report, *Blood on the Streets*, published in 1978, said that Bengali victims of attacks frequently expressed no confidence in the police, considering them to be uninterested or actively biased. It cited one case in 1976 when an Asian was stabbed by a white man in a butcher's shop in Brick Lane. The assailant was held by people in the shop and was taken away by the police, only to be released without charge shortly afterwards, despite the presence of a number of eyewitnesses to the incident. The police asked the assaulted man to drop the case for the sake of 'good community relations' and, when that failed, advised the family to take out a private summons against the man for common assault.

In April 1978, on the way to buy cigarettes for his mother, Kenneth Singh was murdered and his body dumped on a rubbish tip in Plaistow, east London. Altab Ali was murdered in

Whitechapel in May, Ishaque Ali in Hackney in June. Benjamin Thomson and Michael Nathaniel were murdered in Harlesden in July. In September Vernon Brown was murdered in Birmingham, and Amber Ali in Enfield. In December, Michael Ferreira was murdered in Hackney.

Figures given in parliament in 1980 gave some indication of how violence against black people was increasing. According to the Home Office, in 1975 there had been 2690 incidents of assault, robbery or other violent theft where the victims were black. By 1979 this number had risen to 3827.[64] These were the reported incidents and as such will be an underestimate of the true number. In the same year Abdul Aziz was murdered in Peterborough, Kayimarz Anklesaria in east London in August and Sawdagar Khan in Birmingham in the same month.

Another five people were to lose their lives as the result of racial violence in 1980: Mohammed Arif in Burnley and Sewa Singh Sunder in Windsor in January, Famous Mgutshini in London in March, Akhtar Ali Baig in East Ham in July, and Louston Parry in Manchester in September.

In February 1981, the Home Secretary received a delegation from the Joint Committee Against Racialism which presented him with a dossier on racial violence over the previous 18 months, and shortly afterwards an enquiry into racial violence was announced.[65] Given the evidence already available, it is hard to believe that the government was persuaded in its decision by the JCAR document. It seems more likely that it was concerned that racial violence was getting out of hand and, in particular at the black community's readiness to defend itself wherever necessary.

Malcolm Chambers was murdered in Swindon in April and Mian Azim in May. In Coventry, where there had been a dramatic increase in racist violence, Satnam Singh Gill, a 20-year-old student, was stabbed to death in April, and a black doctor, Amil Dharry, was stabbed on 7 June and died ten days later. In Peckham, south London, Fenton Ogbogbo was stabbed to death by three white youths, and in Walthamstow, east London, Parveen Khan and her three children died in a fire widely believed to have been started deliberately. In the same month Charan

Kaur and Poran Singh were murdered in Leeds and in Bradford in November, Mohammed Arif, a taxi driver, had his throat cut.

Black people are also frequently abused and assaulted, and their property attacked by arsonists. The Institute of Race Relations in its evidence to the Royal Commission on Criminal Procedure has cited a number of cases of police unwillingness to provide protection, their refusal to recognise the racial dimension of attacks, delay in responding to incidents, unwillingness to prosecute attackers and hostility to the victims of attacks.[66] Three years later, Francesca Klug, reviewing the literature on the subject, showed that complaints about the police followed a common pattern and generally involved allegations of inactivity, slowness to respond, failure to recognise racist motive and hostility, and occasional verbal and physical abuse by the police towards those complaining.[67]

In response to such criticisms, the report of the Home Office enquiry, *Racial Attacks*, published in November 1981, threw the responsibility for action on racist violence back on to the victims. Black people, the report alleged, ignored the fact that attacks might have occurred on the property of white people too. They did not understand the basic requirements of evidence and they lacked an adequate understanding of police procedures. They were also criticised for not joining the police. (The report said it was a 'natural response' to criticism of the police by black people to question their own willingness to join the police.) Delays or inaction by the police were seen by the report as being unavoidable or due to black people's misunderstanding of procedures, and allegations that people reporting offences were at risk of harassment or arrest by the police were swept aside as 'quite misleading'. On the specific question of the failure of the police to recognise the existence of a racist motive, the study found that the police were *more* likely to ascribe such a motive than the victim of the offence, although it did accept that participation in the study might well have affected police attitudes and, paradoxically, did accept that there was a tendency on the part of the police to underestimate the significance of racial incidents and activities.

It must be emphasised that the Home Office study was *not*

concerned with racial attacks as the term is commonly understood, that is with attacks on black people by whites with some
racist motivation. Instead, the study sought information about
'interracial incidents' – that is where victim and attacker were of
different 'races' – because, the report stated, the Home Secretary
wanted the study to be 'broad based' so that its findings would
command 'the widest possible support'. It is difficult to read this
as meaning anything other than that the government was not
prepared to recognise that racially motivated attacks on black
people are different from others because the phenomenon of
racism underlies such attacks, or that the racist attack acts as
both a reflection and a reinforcer of the racism institutionalised
in society. Instead, the government chose to pander to popular
racism which equates attacks on black people with ordinary
criminal attacks on white people where the attacker is thought to
be black. Right-wing Tory MP Jill Knight, for example, told a
meeting of Conservatives that the Home Office enquiry should
look at the 'increasing harassment of white people by blacks' and
that it should not be 'racist in operation'.[68]

Despite its wrong conception of the problem, the Home Office
study did show that black people were between 50 and 60 times
more likely than whites to be the victims of racially motivated
incidents. It estimated too that in one year about 7000 incidents
would be reported in England and Wales in which there was
either strong evidence or some indication of the presence of a
racial motivation. Such an estimate, it said, was 'almost certainly
to be on the low side'.

The Home Secretary, in a foreword to the report, said that
there were a number of courses of action to be pursued. These
included better liaison between minority communities and the
police, training of police to develop a 'greater sensitivity towards
the phenomenon of racial attacks', and the collection of information about the incidence of racial violence. Ignoring the considerable volume of evidence which had been compiled before the
Home Office survey took place, the Home Secretary maintained
that, 'The failure to appreciate the seriousness of the problem
hitherto has been largely due to a lack of reliable information
about it.'

One year after the publication of the Home Office study, the Runnymede Trust carried out a survey of what changes had taken place in police handling of racial violence since the report was published. It concluded that police forces had not yet shown that they fully understood the significance and seriousness of racial violence and that criticism of police handling of racial violence was still widespread. It reported that the files of the Joint Committee Against Racialism suggested that there had been an increase in the number of planned attacks and that *Searchlight* had reported at least 30 arson attacks. In the East End of London about 200 children were kept from school because of fear that they would be attacked, and there were two apparently racist murders.

In one of these murder cases police quickly ruled out any racial motivation even thought they accepted that the dead man's assailants had shouted ' "Black bastard" and things like that'.[69] In Newham, east London, the local Police Monitoring Project made a number of serious allegations about police attitudes and behaviour. In one case, a black mini-cab driver who lost the sight of one eye in an attack said that when the police came to see him in hospital they were only interested in ascertaining that his driving licence and other documents were in order. Later, when he picked out one of his assailants in an identity parade, the police took no action.[70]

The most telling illustration of the effect – or lack of it – of the Home Office report came during the trial of the Bradford Twelve. In Bradford, 12 Asian youths were charged with conspiracy to endanger life and property, but successfully argued that the petrol bombs they had made were solely for purposes of the self-defence against racial attack. At one point the prosecution in the trial spoke of an 'acceptable level of racial violence' and police officers involved in the investigation having no knowledge of racial violence in the area, even though a recent report had provided a substantial dossier on violence in the city. Nor did the officers know of the Home Office report, even though their force, West Yorkshire, had participated in the study.[71]

It would be hard to overstate the effect of police action or inaction on relations between the police and black people. In the eyes of many black people, the police have singularly failed to afford them the basic protection a police force is supposed to offer the public, while at the same time it has enforced the law in a biased manner against them.

In the 1930s young Jews in London's East End trained themselves in wrestling, boxing, and other self-defence techniques in preparation against fascists. In the 1960s, Asian families in Leamington Spa bought guns to protect themselves after a series of attacks, and only then did the police begin to provide protection. In 1976, after attacks in the Euston and Kings Cross districts of London, black people formed street patrols. These had some success and apprehended several attackers who were handed over to the police. In the same year an Anti-Racist Committee for the Defence of Asians in East London was set up; at about the same time the Bengali Housing Action Group was formed over the issue of racial attacks on housing estates. Nineteen-seventy-eight was a year of extensive racial violence; defence committees were formed in several parts of London and there were many protest marches and demonstrations.[72] On 17 July 1978, Asian traders and factory workers in the Brick Lane area of East London staged a one-day strike to protest against racial violence. On the same day, hundreds of Asians occupied Brick Lane itself in a sit-down protest following the arrest of colleagues during an anti-racist march.

The demonstration by the community of Southall in April 1979 was a statement that they would not be intimidated by racists. Elsewhere communities formed their own defence organisations and held their own protest marches on the issue of racial terror. The single biggest demonstration was the Black People's Day of Action in March 1981. Fifteen thousand people marched from New Cross to central London in protest at the failure of the police and the courts to find the arsonists responsible for the New Cross fire and to protect the black community from racial violence.

The right to defend oneself against attack, although recognised in law, has been so narrowly interpreted as to seem devoid of all substance. A particularly important case was that of the Virk brothers. In April 1977 four brothers were repairing their car outside their home in east London when they were attacked by a gang of white youths. The Virks defended themselves with tools lying to hand and one went to call the police. Yet when the police arrived, the brothers were arrested while their white attackers were allowed to go free. In court Judge Argyle described defence arguments about racial prejudice as 'irrelevant' and rebuked defence lawyers for asking the white attackers whether they were members of the National Front. The four brothers received prison sentences of three months, two years, three years and seven years imprisonment.[73] The three longest sentences were cut by half on appeal. Although Lord Justice Lawton accepted that the appellants were all law-abiding and had been insulted or provoked, the convictions were not reversed.

The reduction of the sentences in the Virk brothers case indicated that some judges were prepared at least to recognise the existence of racial violence; in some other cases black people convicted of carrying weapons were dealt with relatively leniently. Nevertheless, they were still convicted and arguments about self-defence and provocation were usually rejected. The 'right' of self-defence was central, however, in one of the most important trials of black people yet seen in Britain, that of the Bradford Twelve in 1982.

In the summer of 1981, 12 black youths in Bradford were arrested after they had made petrol bombs. They were charged with conspiracy to damage property and endanger the lives of others, and conspiracy to cause grievous bodily harm. They admitted that they had made the bombs but argued that they had done so not for any criminal purpose but to defend themselves and their community from attack. The jury accepted the argument that they could not rely on the police to protect them and accepted too that they had acted reasonably in preparing for self-defence. They were acquitted of all charges. For the time being the right of the black community to defend itself had been established.[74]

The victory of the Bradford Twelve was a clear defeat for the police and government who have regarded self-defence as an interference with what they see as 'their' function. But as A. Sivanandan and Jenny Bourne of the Institute of Race Relations have argued, a community denied the right to be protected has two choices:

It can either submit to indignity, harassment, brutalisation and even murder – or it can defend itself. It is a choice, or rather a 'choicelessness', which no society which prides itself on being free should visit on its citizens, let alone whole communities. For, in the final analysis, the measure of a free society is in the range of effective choices it makes available to its people, irrespective of class, colour or creed.[75]

The policing of black people is racist in many respects. The state has defined black people as a problem whose numbers have to be controlled by immigration laws and the police have had a favourable climate in which to operate. They have offered their own definition of black people as a policing problem which could only be solved by the use of the kind of policing described in this chapter.

# 3. Police public relations

Another response to the presence of black people in Britain has been the creation of structures and programmes to mediate between the police and black people, designed primarily to draw black people into cooperation with the police.

## Community relations

Community relations work with the black community emerged in the late 1950s and 1960s. Until then, every police officer was considered to be a community relations officer in that he or she was expected to maintain and foster good relations with the community. The notion of a distinct concept of community relations in policing would have been anathema to those steeped in traditional policing. What caused the change, according to one theorist of community relations in the Metropolitan Police[1] were not just changes in attitudes to authority – 'something to be questioned rather than respected' – but also increased social mobility both within society and between cultures. This latter, according to Superintendent Lawrence Roach, 'had broken down the homogeneity of the community to the extent that policemen were no longer able to clearly identify with the people they sought to serve'. The new immigrants to Britain did not 'readily recognise or accept the traditional English view of the role of the police', but rather 'tended to regard them as outsiders and as the enforcement arm of the white establishment'. In 1958, therefore, the Metropolitan Police appointed a chief super-intendent to co-ordinate and develop police activity in relation to race. He was the first officer to work specifically in community relations. Ten years later, in 1968, a separate community relations branch was set up to co-ordinate and direct the work of the community liaison officers working at divisional level.

Outside London, a similar picture was developing. In 1967 a circular on *Police and Coloured Communities* was sent by the Home Office to all chief constables and appears to have influenced the setting up of community relations structures in a number of forces. Birmingham, Manchester and Salford city forces, for example, all had full-time community relations officers by the end of the year. Further impetus was provided by the reports of the Home Office working party on police training in race relations, published in 1970, and the report of the Select Committee in 1971, both of which had encouraged greater liaison. In 1976, in response to a Home Office questionnaire on preventive policing, 29 out of 43 forces in England and Wales said that they had some form of community relations work and 17 had separate community relations departments.

The work of community relations officers and departments varies considerably but usually involves liaison with black organisations and police training in race relations. In many areas, community relations officers also sit on the local community relations council. In 1978, 21 out of the 27 CRCs in the London area were attended regularly by the police. In addition, there may be a formal police liaison committee operated by the police and the CRC.

Whatever the work undertaken, community relations has had little if any impact on 'normal' policing, which often simply bypassed community relations or liaison machinery. In 1975, for example, the police liaison committee in the London Borough of Lewisham was not consulted about the use of the Special Patrol Group in the area. In 1977, Brent Community Relations Council broke off formal relations with the police, saying that the community was incensed at the increasing number of black youths who alleged maltreatment by the police. The CRC suspended the liaison committee, banned police from attending general committee meetings and set up a police observation committee to monitor police misconduct.[2] In 1978, in Lambeth, the divisional police commander did not inform the members of the liaison committee about the use of the SPG in the area because he did not trust them. In Hackney, the same year, the community relations council withdrew from the local liaison scheme. A CRC spokesperson said that the number of allegations of police ill-treatment had not declined. 'We got the impression that the police were using it [the liaison committee] to give themselves a better image'.[3] In April 1979, Southall Youth Movement representatives had been told by Chief Inspector Gosse, the community liaison officer, that they could mount a picket against the National Front in Southall; on the day they were moved on by a police officer saying, 'Who the fuck's Gosse? I'm in charge here. Move.'[4]

In 1982, the community relations branch of the Metropolitan Police was not consulted about the release of crime statistics purporting to show disproportionate involvement of black people in street crime. It was not until the Home Office issued a circular in 1981 that community liaison officers had to be informed about any major operations relating to illegal immigrants, although such operations had been taking place since 1973 and had badly damaged relations between the police and black people. Nor has the existence of community liaison officers or community relations branches done anything to ensure better protection of black people from racist attacks and harassment. Nor, indeed, have community relations officers themselves appeared to have any better understanding of the position of black people in British society. For example, Chief Superintendent Carruthers of the City of Glasgow Police Community Involvement Branch returned from a visit to the Indian sub-continent to write a report that reaffirmed police stereotypes of the Asian immigrant as crafty and potentially criminal. Asians, Carruthers said, would 'manipulate the system to the full . . . for example, in immigration and smuggling . . . This type of attitude when transferred to the Welfare State in the United Kingdom could lead to a tendency among some to abuse the system.'[5]

What community relations did achieve was to absolve the police of any understanding of and responsibility to black people and, instead, relegated this to the work of specialist officers. The others could then get on with 'real' policing. Community relations was established to deal with black people's mistrust of the police. Community relations was supposed to break down this mistrust and establish support and consent for the police among the black community. Instead the police located the reason for mistrust and suspicion in the cultural backgrounds and social structures of black people themselves. The police ignored the fact that immigrants from the Caribbean and the West Indies and other ex-colonies had first encountered the British police (or native police trained by the British) as an occupying force and, quite literally, as Superintendent Roach puts it, as 'the enforce-ment arm of the white establishment'. Once in Britain, their experience with the police did little to alter that belief. The police not only helped to enforce laws designed to keep black people out and get rid of some of those already here, but failed to protect them from violence against themselves and their property and enforced laws in a racist way.

Police community relations work has done nothing to show Britain's black citizens why they ought to trust the police. It has co-existed with practices that have affirmed mistrust and made black people a group apart, requiring its own special liaison measures. They were not, however, to remain the only 'group apart'.

As the economic and political crisis of the 1970s deepened and, in particular, as the police began to realise just how much they lacked the support of sections of the public – particularly but not exclusively working-class youth – other special liaison measures were created. Existing ones became more important. These included juvenile liaison schemes, police work in schools and youth clubs, police liaison with social welfare agencies, putting officers back on the beat and 'in touch' with the public. Such moves did not head off rapidly increasing demands for real, political and legal accountability of the police.

However, with an eye to this, Lord Scarman recommended the creation of machinery for 'consultation' between the police and the public, including black people. Such consultation was not to involve formal powers of control over chief constables and other senior officers, backed up by sanctions. It was not a step towards the democratic accountability of the police to the com-munity or its elected representatives. Rather, it was intended to divert demands for accountability by giving the impression that the police were prepared to discuss their tactics – and even some operations – with members of the public. Equally important, consultation was designed to break down the increasing mistrust and hostility felt by many sections of the public to the police. By involving members of the public in policing discussions, the police could implicate them in their own decisions, divert criticism, and achieve legitimation and support for their operations.

### Recruitment of black police

Community relations work is one means by which the police attempted to conciliate and co-opt black people. Equally important have been successive attempts to get black people to join the police and thus show that the force was not an exclusively white organisation. But as there has always been hostility within the police force to community relations work (Scarman noted that, to many in the police, home beat officers were 'hobby bobbies' and not 'real' police officers), so police attitudes to black people joining the force have also been ambivalent. Given the extent of police prejudice, it would be surprising if it had been anything else. But for the sake of their own credibility the police had to be able to show that they were making an effort.

Recruiting more black people into the police is not a new approach. Even Joe Hunte recommended it in 1966 in *Nigger Hunting in England?* So too did *Colour and Citizenship* and the Select Committee in 1972. (With some more thought, one author, John Lambert, told an audience at the Institute of Race Relations in 1970 that it would take more than advertising and promotion of the police service as employment to attract black recruits. Black recruitment on any scale would be a 'sign of improving community race relations, not a cause of their improvement.')[6]

The Metropolitan Police launched a campaign to recruit black people in 1975 at an estimated cost of £25,000, but this was a dismal failure, attracting just 11 applicants, only five of whom actually joined the force. The following year, the parliamentary Select Committee in its report on the West Indian community recommended a study of recruitment of black people. But when this was published it showed what everyone already knew: a strong undercurrent of hostility towards the police, more than any other factor, probably accounted for the failure of suitable people of West Indian origin to come forward as candidates. The Select Committee itself had said several years earlier that, 'Coloured recruitment will not greatly improve while many young West Indians see the police as instruments of oppression.'

In 1981, the number of black officers in the Metropolitan Police was only 132, 0.5 per cent of the total strength, and in the rest of England and Wales there were only 326 black officers, or 0.3 per cent of total strength. Lord Scarman, therefore, recommended yet another 'urgent study' into improving recruitment of black people so that 'the composition of the police fully reflects that of the society the police serve'. Nothing less, he said, will suffice. The resulting study, published in July 1982, recommended in tones of clear urgency that police forces in areas where there was a sizeable black population should advertise the police as a career. They should emphasise special measures available to assist black people to join the force and they should help those who narrowly failed the educational test to succeed if they re-applied. The urgency attached to recruiting more black people into the force was shown by a proposal in Derby by the chief constable that he be allowed to waive the normal educational requirements so as to recruit 12 black officers. In other forces, permission was sought to recruit black officers even though the force was already at full strength. In the West Midlands a recruitment drive aimed at black people was ordered in January 1982, and in South Yorkshire, where there were only three black officers in the force of 2000, an assistant chief constable and chief superintendent were despatched to the United States to study recruitment strategies there.

The police were therefore taking Scarman's message to heart, although the chair of the constables' group of the Police Federation strongly criticised any form of what he saw as 'positive discrimination'.[7] Such measures did appear to have some success and the Metropolitan Police claimed in October 1982 that the number of black applicants to join the police had more than doubled over the previous year. But the number of actual recruits was still tiny, only 46, while the proportion of black applicants who actually joined the police declined from 12 per cent in 1981 to 8.6 per cent in 1982.[8]

It seems unlikely that the various special measures now being taken will bring about any significant change while the actual practices of the police remain unchanged. Even if more black people were to join the police, this in itself would be unlikely to make any significant difference to the policing of black people. It has not done so in the United States. Rather, it seems, a 'multi-racial' police force would give the police an increased legitimacy and an acceptable face in the policing of black people, without in any way altering the content of that policing.

## Police training

Finally, we must consider the question of police training in 'race relations', a subject to which considerable importance has been attached over the years, especially in the aftermath of the 1981 riots and in the light of the Scarman report. In 1970 John Lambert, author of *Crime, the Police and Race Relations*, spoke on policing at the Institute of Race Relations. Lambert argued that there was little to be gained from lecturing the police against prejudice if their work allowed an extension of their attitudes into their actions. What needed to be explored in police training and beyond was *how* attitudes were expressed and perceived and what handling people in a multi-racial context actually meant. What also needed to be looked at was how police organisation inhibited reform through training, so that training was given a low priority and its effects were severely limited because it could not counter entrenched police attitudes. These were perceptive remarks, borne out by subsequent research and developments. They were also consistently ignored by the police.

A Home Office working party on police training in race relations had been set up in 1970. Composed of Home Office officials and police officers, the working party argued that the police must understand various groups in society and the (unspecified) 'problems of immigrant settlement'. Friction between the police and black people was due to the 'social tensions' that hampered 'absorption', combined with mutual misunderstanding between the two groups. The problem was therefore one of understanding and communication, and to this end the working party recommended that training in race relations should help the police understand the background of minority groups and white attitudes and behaviour in order 'to cope with the problems created by the concentration of coloured people in our cities'. When the 1972 Select Committee report recommended that these proposals be implemented, the government's response was that implementation was a matter for individual chief constables.

Whatever changes have been made in police training in race, they do not seem to have had any impact on policing itself and they certainly have not led to any less criticism of the police by black people. Police training appears to have only a short-term liberalising effect on the attitudes of police officers, and a later study from the Home Office concluded that police training in race relations had 'no detailed and consistent goals'. The author, Peter Southgate, carrying out his research in Leeds, found that few officers remembered anything they had been taught, while others denied they had ever received such training. Police officers were moulded only by experience, which they regarded as real, not by what they learned in the classroom. Training also had apparently little impact on racist attitudes and the use of racist stereotypes among police officers. Officers frequently used offensive language about black people without any overt criticism from senior officers. In addition, Southgate's findings confirmed those of the Gorman and Colman research (discussed in chapter 4) that any impact training might have was countered by the informal police subculture.[9]

The problem, however, goes deeper than this. Its roots lie in the purpose of police training in community relations. Superintendent Roach, in his article on the Metropolitan Police community relations branch, says that it is not part of such training to attempt 'to "convert" an officer to a particular point of view or to change personal or political opinions'. The purpose is to 'inculcate an understanding of the strategic importance of good police/community relations and to set the high standards of professional conduct needed to achieve that objective'. The case against this approach has most been most cogently expressed by the Institute of Race Relations that,

> unless the individual officer . . . regards it as his function to serve and protect the black community as much as the white, to keep the peace equally for black and white, the problems . . . cannot begin to be tackled effectively. Education is here of paramount importance, but an education which acknowledges the reality and pervasiveness of racism and which looks at the nature of racial violence. To pay lip-service to a concept of multi-racialism, by attempting for example to gloss over the racist dimension of attacks against black people, serves only to heighten their fear and distrust.[10]

When an attempt was made at developing a course with an anti-racist component at the Metropolitan Police training school at Hendon, north London, it was met with considerable opposition both from the police and some of the academic staff. One of those involved, Christine Anketell, a black teacher, said that throughout the dispute the only support came from a handful of the academic staff while 'every form of institutional racialism was brought to bear upon us to prevent us from running the course.' These included timetable obstacles, open condemnation, requests for 'joint working parties' even after the course had been accepted by the academic board, and some verbal abuse. The police eventually dropped a crucial part of the course, which led one of the lecturers, John Fernandes, to release to the media racist essays written by cadets (see chapter 4). Anketell concluded that, 'the police really had no commitment to the course. All they wanted was "window dressing" with a couple of "Uncle Toms" in order to convince the public that police and cadet training methods had been changed following the Scarman report.'[11]

The police approach – community relations work, recruitment of black people, training in race relations – avoids the real issue of racism: racism in society and in the police force itself. The problem, according to the police, lies in lack of knowledge, misunderstandings and difficulties in communication. But community relations work is marginal and generally ignored by mainstream policing. It has no impact on how the policing of black communities is carried out. Recruitment of black people into the police has been singularly unsuccessful, and training has been inconsistent and its effects short-lived. Clearly then, this approach has failed on both levels, having no impact on the routine racist policing of black people and, in an ideological sense, failing to win over the hearts and minds of black people to the police cause.

# 4. Understanding police racism

There are three reasons for racist policing. Firstly, there is the existence within the police of individuals who are themselves racist. Secondly, the police operate in the context of institutionalised racism where black people are, by definition, a policing problem. Thirdly, there is the more general question of the wider changes in British society in the past two decades and the accompanying changes in policing.

## Police prejudice

There can be no doubt that police officers are racist. The police themselves accept that it is so, and argue that the police are only a cross-section and therefore reflect the make-up of that society. The argument is, of course, put forward precisely to excuse the existence of racism within the police, but, as Stuart Hall has pointed out, it is difficult to imagine that a similar argument would be used to justify the existence within the police of criminals who are also part of the society from which the police are drawn.[1]

In fact, prejudice in the police is certainly far more extensive than the police (and Lord Scarman who, contrary to much of the evidence he claimed to have read, considered that prejudice was only 'occasionally' manifest on the streets by a 'few officers') would have us believe. Tony Judge, himself a former police officer and now editor of *Police*, the Police Federation journal, described a number of rank-and-file police views in his book on the British police, *A Man Apart*.[2] Judge reported statements such as black people 'just hate policemen. They take it in with their mothers milk' (a Birmingham constable); 'It used to be a good neighbourhood. Then we got all those wogs and just look at it' (officer in Chapeltown, Leeds); 'They all know about complaints against the police, I can tell you. Soon as you speak to one he's on at you. "Don't you touch me copper, what's your number, man?" I'll tell you this, I've never backed down to a white man when I've been in this uniform, and I'm not backing down to a black' (sergeant in Birmingham); 'They complain out of force of habit . . . They'll lie from morning till night, and they know it's lies' (a London detective). 'Powell is the only politician who tells the truth,' was, said Judge, 'a statement I have heard often enough from many policemen.'

The results of such beliefs, when the police actually deal with black people, have been shown earlier in this book. In addition, psychological research has found extensive prejudice. Two researchers from the Department of Social Psychology at Leicester University (one of them a police officer) concluded that the police force attracted conservative and authoritarian personalities and that basic training had only a temporary liberalising effect on racial prejudice. (The study was the first in Britain to use a control group for purposes of comparison and confirms other, more limited, research.) The researchers found that the greatest degree of prejudice and intolerance was found in probationer constables in relation to black people, who were variously described as 'smelly', 'dirty', 'uneducated', 'troublesome', 'disrespectful of the law' and as taking over the country. Continued service in the police, they concluded, resulted in increasingly illiberal and intolerant attitudes towards black people.[3]

One must, therefore, be pessimistic about the future. Here are some extracts, quoted exactly, from essays written in 1982 by police cadets at the Metropolitan Police Training School at Hendon. The subject they were asked to write about was 'Blacks in Britain':

Blacks in Britain are a pest . . . quite frankly I don't have any liking whatsoever for wogs, nig nogs and Pakies . . . They are by nature, unintelegent and can't at all be educated suficiently to live in a civilised society of the Western world.

It makes me cringe when I see a black bloke going out with a white woman . . . England is a traditionally white country and that is how it should stay, the blacks must accept that if they are to live in this country they must fall in line under white British dictators and not try and run the country themselves from the backstreet slums.

I think that blacks are alright. I am not partricaly prejudice against them but on certain occasions I have less patients with them than perhaps one of my own race. Especially at the moment with the present Falklands Crisis, the coloureds wish to be taken in as a part of the British community and yet when a crisis arises the are just sitting back. I do not think I have seen one coloured person in the task force.

I think all blacks are pains and should be expelled from our society.[4]

The release of these essays to the media by one of the lecturers at the training school might reasonably have been expected to cause something of a storm about police attitudes, especially since 90 per cent of all cadets go on to become police officers. What happened was quite different. The police and some of the media attempted to play down the seriousness of the remarks, some even going so far as to describe them as 'jokes'. The lecturer who leaked the essays, John Fernandes, was required to leave the school by its officer in charge, Commander Wells, and the incident brought to light the obstruction and watering down the police of the 'multi-cultural' component of the course. The incident illustrated the reality of police 'commitment' to weeding out racists, to recognising the multi-racial nature of society, and of equal policing for all.

### Institutional racism

It would be wrong to see the prejudice of individual police officers as the only or even the main explanation for racist policing, just as it would be wrong to explain the position of black people in Britain today as the result of prejudiced individuals.

Even if racialism within the police were dealt with tomorrow, the police would still be operating within a racist context. The British state defined black people as a problem, both through immigration laws to keep them out, and through measures of 'integration' designed to manage the 'problem' already here. In this management of the 'black problem' the police have played a key role. They have not merely enforced the laws of the state against black people. They have not acted as mere servants of the state, doing what was asked of them. They offered their own definition of black people as a policing problem, a definition which both reflected the institutionalised racism of the state and society at large and reinforced it.

The police have often denied that there was any problem at all, at least any problem that could not easily be sorted out. Thus Geoffrey Dear, later to become Deputy Assistant Commissioner in the Metropolitan Police, wrote in 1972 that the problems were simply those of misunderstanding, particularly as immigrants brought with them 'preconceived ideas and mental images of the police'. While there had been a number of 'lamentable instances of police prejudice and insensitivity', black people focussed their grievances on the police because of the 'race relations industry'. Dear then went on to accept that the vast amount of work in this field was of the highest quality and done by people with the 'highest possible motives'. The task for the police was therefore to distinguish between 'those with a genuine message or with sound advice on one hand, and those with dubious arguments or with malicious or politically inspired motives on the other'. Dear had therefore provided the police with a justification for listening to what they wanted to hear and ignoring what they disliked.[5]

Dear's argument reflected those given by police to the Select Committee around the same time. These blamed friction between the police and black people on 'militants' and the 'underground press'. The Police Federation, claiming that it had been 'second to none' in its efforts to help immigrants, blamed immigrant leaders who 'could do much more to foster contact between the police and black people'. As the process of portraying the black population as criminal got under way, this line of thinking declined in importance, but it was still there to be used whenever necessary. Thus, in 1980 the Metropolitan Police Commissioner, Sir David McNee, claimed that 'myth and rumour' prevailed about relations between the police and black people and the situation was therefore ready made for extremists to exploit. There were also 'those with apparent good intent who by injudicious criticisms undermine the maintenance of the law'. McNee's attack was taken up the following year by another leading chief constable, James Anderton. His main target was also the 'race relations industry' whose 'solicitous attention' to black people was 'fast becoming counter-productive'. The original ideals, Anderton claimed, had got lost in a 'web of political intrigue and opportunism'. Again Anderton sought to distinguish the goodies whose genuine desire was nullified by the baddies 'who blatantly employ the system as a catalyst for promoting racial disharmony and antagonising the police'.

This kind of 'argument' which sought to avoid the question of racism and which exculpated the police by blaming 'outsiders', from 'black power activists' to the 'race relations industry', had by this time become secondary. It was certainly useful to attack those in the 'race industry' who sided with black people; McNee, for example, had singled out the church in his 1980 speech. But as far as the black community itself was concerned, the police had embarked on the more effective strategy of portraying them as a criminal community.

When the Select Committee on Race Relations and Immigration was looking into relations between the police and black people in 1971–72, police forces, almost without exception, pointed to the fact that black people were no more likely to be involved in crime than were white people. Indeed, the chief constable of Lancashire told the Committee that there had been no call to keep separate statistics of black and white crime and said that the mere keeping of such statistics 'would tend to indicate a belief that race (or colour, which is really the crux of the situation) has a bearing on criminal propensity, which is not an acceptable proposition to the unbiased mind.' Such laudable attitudes were, however, ignored and, even as the Lancashire chief constable spoke, others within the police moved to give a different picture. A south London detective told the *Guardian* in

August 1971 that 'a good seven out of ten street robbers that we pick up have an immigrant background; they are usually from the West Indies, Europe or Ireland. They don't include Indians and Pakistanis, they are usually very law-abiding people and areas in which they settle are in my experience very law-abiding.'[6] In west London, a special study carried out by B Division of the Metropolitan Police, which covers Notting Hill, claimed that black people made up 12 per cent of the area's population but that they constituted 15.3 per cent of those charged in Notting Hill and 11.6 in Notting Dale. In 1971, 30 out of 38 robberies in the area were alleged to have been committed by black people.

By late 1972 a national panic had arisen over the question of 'mugging', a new name for the old offence of street robbery, but one which now had an explicitly racial connotation. 'Muggers' was equated with 'black', and special police 'anti-mugging' squads harassed and intimidated black youths as suspected 'muggers'. The panic – media-led and police-fed – reached its vengeful height in March 1973 when three youths, one Cypriot, one with a West Indian father, and one white, were ordered to be detained, two for ten years and one for 20 years, for assaulting and robbing a man in Handsworth, Birmingham.

This move towards the portrayal of black people, especially West Indian youths, as criminals, was given added weight by sociologists and journalists. In the former category, John Brown, a sociologist with strong connections with the police, published his *Theory of Police-Immigrant Relations* in 1974. Brown's view of the black community is one of racist stereotypes. In talking about the 'cultures and conditions of local immigrant groups' (factor 3 in his list of ten which determine the state of relations between the police and black people), 'Asian crime' was seen as being 'more cerebral, sophisticated and organised than West Indian crime'. It was underground, 'only glimpses showing even to police eyes', as exemplified, of course, in illegal immigration. Offers of bribes to police officers by Asians were, Brown claimed, 'commonplace'. West Indian experience, on the other hand, created 'a stereotype of deprivation' – a child is brought up by grandparents in the West Indies, comes later to the UK to join the mother, who by this time 'may have changed partners'; the child then competes for affection with other children, finds it difficult to cope with a cold, unfamiliar urban world and an unfamiliar school where ' "free expression" replaces rote learning, and where discipline seems non-existent'. The West Indian lacks the discipline, drive and human support of the Asian. The predisposition to crime is obvious. In addition to all this, 'black power' groups exploit the situation. The concept of 'black community', Brown sneered, was of 'dubious reality' and the drive of black power for dignity and equality merged into 'incitements to destruction and violence'.

Derek Humphry, the *Sunday Times* reporter on race, wrote in January 1975 of the 'Danger signals from the streets of Lambeth', reporting on a police study which claimed that 80 per cent of street crime was committed by black people, while 85 per cent of the victims were white. 'Soaring street crime', the report claimed, 'is caused by widespread alienation of West Indian youngsters from white society' and Humphry claimed that there were West Indians between the ages of 8 and 25 who existed solely on the proceeds of street crime.[7]

Humphry had prefaced his report with a hope that the facts he reported would not be used to feed prejudice, but in fact the *Sunday Times* story became the start of a much stronger strategy by the police and the press to portray the black community as criminal. By 1976 the process was well under way. Enoch Powell, referring to mugging, told a Police Federation seminar in April that 'To use a crude but effective word for it – it is racial,'[8] a judgement on which the *Daily Telegraph* in an editorial the following day commented, 'Mr Powell was right to remind us of the unpleasant facts about race and violent crime in London.' In October the Metropolitan Police issued figures claiming that 80 per cent of muggings in the Peckham area of south London were by black people, while the 'vast majority' of victims were white. The *Sunday Telegraph* wrote in an editorial:

Reports on mugging from all parts of London which will reach Scotland Yard tomorrow from its divisional detectives show that crime has greatly increased. In Brixton there have been 800 muggings so far this year, in Lewisham 432 and in Notting

Hill 500, as well as the 339 announced in Peckham earlier last week. The problem extends to Haringey, Hammersmith, Hackney, Islington, Southwark and Tower Hamlets.[9]

The paper did not need to add that all these areas had large concentrations of black people.

In the same year, the Metropolitan Police submitted its evidence to the Select Committee on Race Relations and Immigration which was now looking at the West Indian community. The Met drew attention to the perceived link between West Indians and street crime, arguing that 'London's black citizens, among whom those of West Indian origin predominate, are disproportionately involved in many forms of crime.' The Select Committee in its report in 1977 said that it found 'no evidence available to justify any firm conclusions about the relative involvement of West Indians in crime'. But in a sense this hardly mattered, for the police, through the press, had established their point in the common consciousness. Street crime was firmly established as a black activity against white people. In a remark on the evidence to the Select Committee in his report for the year, the Metropolitan Police Commissioner noted that, 'as might have been expected, parts of that evidence have since been misused by some as racist propaganda. Such is the dilemma of public debate.'

John Brown, the author of *A Theory of Police-Immigrant Relations* discussed earlier, had been asked to examine relations between the police and black people in Handsworth. His report, *Shades of Grey*, published in 1979, failed to answer the many allegations made against the police and instead sought to blame a 'couple of hundred "hard-core" Dreadlocks who now form a criminalised sub-culture' for threatening the peace of other citizens and making life difficult for the police.

The police themselves were managing to fulfil their own prophecies and assertions. By over-policing black areas and black events they were able to cause reactions they could then use to justify even harsher policing. Nowhere was this clearer than in the policing of the Notting Hill Carnival in 1976 when the aggressive presence of an unprecedented number of police provoked many of those present. The resulting disorder became a justification for even greater numbers of police at the Carnival in future years. The same was true of other events and in other areas. The Metropolitan Police themselves had complained to the Select Committee in 1976 of the

> potentiality for conflict which is inherent in every law enforcement situation between police and West Indians . . . Recently there has been a growth in the tendency for members of London's West Indian communities to combine against police by interfering with police officers who are effecting the arrest of a black person or who are in some way enforcing the law in situations which involve black people. In the last 12 months forty such incidents have been recorded. Each carries a potential for large scale disorder.

The police, therefore, had a ready-made justification for their actions against black people – they were more involved in crime and, when caught, joined together to fight the police. Special measures were therefore necessary.

But the reaction to such 'special measures' could easily get out of hand. When on occasions it did, the police were called to account and had to explain their actions. Thus, the 1981 riots were clearly seen as a response to police behaviour over a number of years, even if few were going to say so, for fear of being seen to 'condone' the rioters and criticise the police. The British police had been threatened in a way unique in modern times, and the singularity of that threat demanded examination of the policing methods which had given rise to it. The criticism that followed from the liberal establishment centred around Lord Scarman's report.

Scarman concurred with the statement made by the Prime Minister at the time of the first Brixton riots in April, that 'Nothing . . . can excuse the unlawful behaviour of the rioters.' He rejected views that the disorders had been caused by oppressive policing over a period of years and in particular by the harassment of young blacks on the streets. He rejected too the view that the disorders were a protest against society by people deeply deprived and frustrated. Each view, he said, even if correct, 'would be an over-simplification of a complex situation.

If either view should be true, it would not be the whole truth'.[10]

Scarman sought to locate the disorders in their social, economic and political context – of acute deprivation, discrimination and political insecurity. Such, said Scarman, encouraged protest on the streets and a drift into crime: 'The recipe for a clash with the police is therefore ready mixed.' None of this was a *cause* of the disorders but it was, Scarman claimed, a set of social conditions which 'create a *predisposition* towards violent protest' (emphasis added).[11]

Scarman proceeded to seek the roots of the problem not only in social and economic factors, but in a pathology of the West Indian family (including the absence of fathers, mothers going out to work, challenges to discipline and authority) and in the undefined 'problem' of policing a multi-racial society. In the course of this discussion, Scarman rejected the idea that institutionalised racism existed in Britain, 'if by that is meant it is a society which knowingly, as a matter of course, discriminates against black people'.

In dealing with the immediate background to the disorders, Scarman had no doubt that a significant cause of the hostility felt by the community towards the police was a loss of confidence in the police by significant sections of the local public, leading to a serious breakdown in police/public relations. The factors leading to this breakdown were identified as: the collapse of the police liaison committee in 1979; the use of 'hard' policing, including the use of the SPG; the use of laws like sus, which were especially aimed at street crime; distrust of the police complaints system; and unlawful and racially prejudiced conduct by police officers.

But having identified these factors, Scarman went on to say that the decision of the community relations council in Lambeth to abandon the police liaison committee had been wrong. He also said that the working party enquiry into police/public relations set up by Lambeth Borough Council had succeeded 'only in worsening community relations with the police', even though he accepted that the report had reflected attitudes and beliefs widely held in the area.

Scarman unequivocally rejected criticism of the 'integrity and impartiality' of the senior officers of the police. Many of those who gave evidence to the enquiry had argued that the riots had been provoked by harassment of black people by a racist police force which was unaccountable to the community. Scarman rejected this and maintained that racial prejudice was manifested only 'occasionally in the behaviour of a few officers on the streets'. Such bias, he said, was not to be found among senior officers.

Nevertheless, Scarman did accept that some of the allegations of harassment were true: 'the weight of criticism and complaint against the police is so considerable that it alone must give cause for concern.'[12] But he ascribed some of this criticism to 'gossip and rumour', saying that there must be a temptation for every young criminal stopped or arrested to allege misconduct by the police.

In conclusion, Scarman argued that the police had to carry 'some responsibility' for the outbreak of disorder but the primary responsibility was placed on the community itself.

The Scarman report made a large number of recommendations in policing, law reform and social policy. These included an urgent study of the ways in which recruitment of black people into the police might be increased, including the possible provision of special educational training; the doubling of initial police training to six months with greater attention paid to the prevention of disorder and 'the understanding of the cultural backgrounds and attitudes found in a multi-racial society'; and the creation of a police disciplinary offence of racially prejudiced or discriminatory behaviour, the normal punishment for which should be dismissal.

On policing methods, Scarman advocated greater use of foot patrols alongside mobile patrols, but these would be backed up by effective reinforcement arrangements, increased police training in the handling of disorder, and more effective protective clothing and equipment, including CS gas, plastic bullets and water cannon. Scarman also recommended the independent investigation of all but frivolous complaints against the police, but firmly rejected arguments for greater accountability of the police to the public, advocating instead the establishment of better 'consultative arrangements'.

Overall the Report exonerated the police, but even its muted criticism proved too much for police hardliners. Shortly after the Report was published the Metropolitan Police launched its counter offensive. On 21 January 1982 the *Daily Mail* reported that Deputy Assistant Commissioner Gilbert Kelland (who was to announce the criminal statistics in March) had had a meeting with divisional commanders and told them that there should be no let-up in operations against muggers just because of the Scarman Report's criticism of Operation Swamp '81. From then on, the press kept up its coverage, based solely on police reports, of how Scarman had 'hampered' the police, how 'muggings' were increasing and how the streets of London were unsafe because of black 'muggers'. On 10 March the Metropolitan Police issued figures purporting to to show that black people were disproportionately involved in street crime. The criminal statistics highlighted two things. Firstly, between 1980 and 1981 there was a rise in serious crime of 8 per cent. Secondly, there was a reported increase in robbery and other violent theft and an alleged disproportionate involvement of black people in this kind of crime. The press focussed on the latter especially, because the police had provided a breakdown on the appearance of assailants. This showed 4967 as white and 10,399 as coloured. The *Daily Mail* headlined its report on the statistics, 'Violence double that by whites, Yard reveal'.[13] The Fleet Street papers used the figures to show that 'mugging' was on the increase.

'Mugging', however, is not an offence known in law and the term is not normally used by the police. The Metropolitan Police statistics for robbery and other violent theft included only 5889 incidents that would popularly be called 'muggings', that is, thefts in the street with some violence. These accounted for only 31 per cent of all robbery and other violent thefts, and only 0.9 per cent of all serious recorded offences.

The use of race in the statistics was confined to robbery and other violent thefts and was not used in any other category. Only 'muggings' were portrayed as black crimes. The police claimed that race was categorised according to the perception of the victim. In at least one case, the assailant was recorded as black even though the victim told a TV journalist that she had been struck from behind and was too stunned to see her attacker. How the assailant came to be classified as black is not known, nor is the number of similar cases.[14] The Metropolitan Police statistics concentrated on one category of crime which represented only 3 per cent of all serious reported crime. The fact that the number of homicides had fallen by 36 per cent on the previous year was ignored as was the fact that the number of assaults had risen only slightly and would probably have remained at their 1980 level if the Brixton riots had not occurred.

The police and media disregarded all the normal qualifications and warnings about criminal statistics: that they deal only with reported crime, generally reckoned to be a small fraction of all crime; that the reporting of crime can rise without an increase in the number of actual offences, for example, where there is publicity around a particular offence; and that the number of reported crimes can rise as a result of increased police activity or presence in an area. The police themselves are well aware of such important qualifications. The chief constable of Greater Manchester, James Anderton, had told the Manchester Statistical Society, 'What precisely do the statistics tell us about the state of criminality in the nation and what do they suggest should be done about it? Very little, is the answer I would give.'[15] Only a month before the release of the statistics, the Police Federation magazine *Police* had said that: 'No informed person regards the existing criminal statistics as the most reliable indicator of the state of crime.'[16]

The picture presented was partial, dishonest and statistically quite unsound,[17] but the police, once again, had achieved their purpose. As solicitor Gareth Pierce wrote, the police had revealed their strongest weapon, 'not CS gas or plastic bullets, the deployment of which causes some public concern, but effective control of a willing and uncritical press, which causes none.'[18] They had provided, by means of the press, a justification for their favoured tactics in the policing of black people. They had established, yet again, the equation of street crime and black people.

A more subtle approach was being developed, intentionally or unintentionally, and one that could count on the support of some supposed liberals. Scarman, in his report, had spoken of the problem of 'policing a multi-racial community'. It was not the first time this expression had been used. Two years before, Metropolitan Police Commissioner Sir David McNee had asserted that:

> Policing a multi-racial society is putting the fabric of our policing philosophy under greater stress than at any time since the years immediately after the Metropolitan Police was established in 1829.[19]

After Scarman, however, the phrase and its underlying assumptions slipped into common parlance, to become a standard concept in 'liberal' discussions about policing after the riots. It reveals a racism more subtle than that of the police, racism because the use of 'multi-racial' in this context can mean only one thing. If policing in itself is the problem then the use of 'multi-racial' is irrelevant and redundant. But if 'multi-racial' has a function then what the phrase means is that the multi-racial nature of society is a problem, at least for the police. To put it crudely, the phrase means that the presence of black people is a problem for the police. The black community is seen as being criminal or supportive of criminality in that, the argument goes, it does not want the law enforced against black people. This assumption is implicit in Scarman's description of what he saw as the 'policing dilemma' of how to cope with crime ('particularly . . . street robbery') and at the same time retain the confidence of all sections of the community, 'especially ethnic minority groups'.[20]

What this ignores, of course, is that the issue has never been whether the police should enforce the law and protect people and their property. It has never been that black people want to be treated differently. The issue is, and has been, the failure of the police to protect black communities from racist violence and harassment, the portrayal of a community, a whole people, as criminal, the kind of laws the police choose to enforce, the ways in which these laws are enforced, and the purpose of that law enforcement. The problem of policing a multi-racial society is not black people, but racist policing.

## Conclusion

The policing of black people cannot be seen in isolation. It does not exist on its own but forms part of the policing of working-class communities generally. The 1970s were the years of technical changes in policing and police methods, the era of the technological cop. They were also the years of the social, economic and political crisis in which Britain found itself, transforming the nature of society, bringing about a generation that, in employment prospects, had no future. The deprivations of this period were nothing new to black people. They had known unemployment such as the white working class of the post-war years had not seen, they had lived in the decayed and decaying areas of the inner cities, and they had known the authoritarian state response to their presence – the rigours of immigration control, external and internal, the heavy-handed policing of their communities, the blind eye turned to racism and its violent manifestations. What was different about the 1970s was that the white working class too was hit by unemployment, not the short term unemployment of before, but the permanent, structural unemployment where jobs disappeared for ever.

The police have the task of controlling the social effects of the economic crisis. They might not be able to alleviate the effects, but they could certainly try to contain it in the inner city areas. It is in this context that one has to understand recent police awareness of *social* problems. For the continued growth of social problems made containment of discontent an increasingly difficult task. And so it finally proved in the summer of 1981, when white joined black on the streets of 30 towns and cities up and down the country to vent their anger on the police. It was the police who were, and are, policing the crisis not, as they would have us believe, in the sense that they simply 'pick up the pieces' or deal with the social effects of unemployment and poverty, but in the sense that they themselves, through their policies, strategies, tactics and operations, defined the 'policing problem' and its solution. The police, in other words, are not simply the most readily accessible *symbol* of authority of the state, but its clearest expression in the lives of the 'never employed'.[21]

# 5. Racism and the courts

Every judge on his appointment discards all politics and prejudices. You need have no fear. The Judges of England have always in the past – and always will – be vigilant in guarding our freedoms. Someone must be trusted. Let it be the judges.

Lord Denning, Dimbleby Lecture, 1980

It's no use talking to me about justice 'cos there ain't none. What justice do we get from white society? None at all: that's straight . . . I don't trust anyone in court.

Black youth, quoted in *New Society*, 24 February 1980

Liberal and conservative notions of the courts and the legal system hold that they are bulwarks between executive and administrative authority and the citizen, that the courts act as the protectors of the citizen against the unfair or arbitrary denial of rights and as impartial arbiters in legal disputes. Scrutiny shows however that judges, far from discarding their politics and prejudices when they put on wigs or gowns, take their attitudes into court and make decisions on the basis of their beliefs and prejudices. This chapter sets out to show how the judges and the courts have operated in their dealings with black people and how this relationship has reflected and affirmed the racism of society in general and the criminal justice system in particular.

## Immigration law: undermining the settled[1]

Judges in the superior courts have considerable power in determining the limits and scope of laws passed by parliament. Just how far black people could trust the judges was shown very soon after the Immigration Act 1971 came into force in January 1973. The case of *Azam* reached the House of Lords in June 1973. The Home Office alleged that Azam was an illegal entrant even though he had come into the country before 1 January 1973 when the law came into force and even though he had not been convicted within the six month period required by the previous law. The House of Lords ruled in favour of the Home Office and made a criminal of Azam and of an uncertain number of people in a similar position. The case involved a second legal point of some importance: whether the appellant could be regarded as 'settled' in the UK when the 1971 Act came into force. If so, he could not be deported. Again, the House of Lords ruled in favour of the Home Office and held that the 1971 Act in this respect was retrospective, that is, the statute covered situations extant before it came into force. Immigrants held to have entered illegally could thus be removed under the administrative powers of the 1971 Act even though previous law stated that they were immune from prosecution and deportation. The *Azam* decision was the first of many to extend considerably the scope of the law beyond that envisaged by most MPs when it was being discussed and passed. Whether Home Office officials at the time appreciated the possible scope of the law we do not know. In any case, the courts were not bound by what was thought or said in parliament and could extend the law as they saw fit regardless of the apparent intention of parliament.

A limited amnesty was announced by the newly elected Labour government in 1974 to deal with the effects of the *Azam* decision. The amnesty and its extension in 1978 were limited in scope and in 1975 the Court of Appeal held that it conferred no rights but simply amounted to an intention by the government to mitigate the effects of the law.

For the early years of the operation of the 1971 Immigration Act it was assumed that illegal immigrants were those who avoided immigration controls altogether, as was the case under previous laws. The Act itself defined an illegal entrant as someone who unlawfully entered or tried to enter in breach of a deportation order or of the immigration laws. During the debates on the new law the Home Secretary, Reginald Maudling, had spoken of those who 'sneak across the beaches late at night'. The meaning of illegal entry seemed fairly clear. At least it did until 1976 when the case of *Maqbool Hussain* reached the courts. Then, and in the case of *Bangoo* a few months later, the Home Office argued that deception also amounted to illegal entry. In both cases, the immigrants admitted their deceit and accepted that this made their entry illegal. The issue was not therefore tested and the novelty of the Home Office interpretation of the law was not adequately appreciated.

In the same year, the House of Lords curtailed the appeal rights of the many people who had been allowed into the UK for a limited period. In the case of *Suthendran* it was held that a person with limited permission to remain in the UK must make an application to the Home Office for an extension of the period of stay before the existing period has expired. There is no right of appeal against a refusal to extend the period where the application is made too late. Before this decision the Home Office had generally interpreted the Act broadly and had not taken action against those who had appealed out of time. Following the decision, however, the Home Office changed its practice and restricted applications for appeal to those made within 28 days of refusal of an extension, where the application for extension had been made during the period of leave.

Alongside such decisions, which extended the scope of the law, the courts reduced the ability of people detained as illegal entrants to challenge their detention. The 1971 Act took away the right of an illegal entrant to appeal to an immigration adjudicator or to the Immigration Appeal Tribunal. Detained immigrants had therefore to rely on the ancient remedy of *habeas corpus*. An application for *habeas corpus* is open to anyone detained without permission of the courts. The detained person must be released unless police or prison officials can satisfy the court that continued temporary imprisonment is justified. For centuries, the writ has been the pride of constitutional lawyers. The Victorian constitutional writer, A. V. Dicey, for example, thought it 'worth a hundred constitutional articles guaranteeing individual liberty' while in current times the Supreme Court

Practice (the lawyers' bible of court procedure) holds it 'of the highest constitutional importance, for by it the liberty of the subject is vindicated and his release from any manner of unjustifiable detention assured'.[2] One must qualify such praise however, for, as one leading immigration lawyer has pointed out, the attributes of *habeas corpus* are unimportant 'unless the judges before whom the applications are brought are prepared to defend individual liberty against encroaching executive power. On this the history of *habeas corpus* is decidedly mixed'.

In 1978 when Safdar Hussain applied for *habeas corpus* the Court of Appeal refused to enquire into the circumstances of his detention. It was enough, the court said, if the Home Secretary had reasonable grounds for his belief that Hussain was an illegal entrant and therefore liable to detention. The thinking behind the decision was followed by the Court of Appeal in the case of *Choudhary* in the same year and was approved by the House of Lords two years later in the case of *Zamir*. The thrust of these decisions was that immigrants could be detained and removed from the UK not for what they had done but for what the Home Secretary thought they had done. If the minister's decision appeared 'reasonable', the courts would not interfere. In *Safdar Hussain*'s case it was alleged that the immigrant had lied to the immigration officer. The definition of illegal entrant was therefore now wider than that of those who 'sneak across the beaches'. But even this was superseded two years later, in what Lord Widgery described as a 'modest step foward', in the case of *Zamir*.

Zamir was 15 when an application was made on his behalf to join his father in the UK. His entry depended on his being a dependent son, that is, he had to be under 18 or, if over 18, unmarried. Zamir's application took three years to be processed and, after his visa was issued but before he left for the UK, he married. Zamir passed through immigration control and answered all questions truthfully. He was not questioned about his marital status. Two years after arriving in the UK he applied for his wife to join him. He was interviewed and arrested as an illegal entrant on the grounds that had the immigration officer known of his marriage he would have refused him entry. There is no evidence that Zamir understood the significance of his marriage but as far as the courts were concerned this was irrelevant. Lord Widgery in the Divisional Court ruled that Zamir should have disclosed to the immigration officer any change in his circumstances which 'he knew or ought to have known' was material and Lord Wilberforce in the House of Lords agreed saying that an immigrant owed 'a positive duty of candour on all material facts which denote a change of circumstances since the issue of the entry clearance'.

In the wake of such decisions came a trail of people, long settled in the UK, threatened with removal as illegal entrants. They included people who had entered the country on work permits but had not declared the existence of children; other work permit holders whose references were false, even though this was the work of unscrupulous employment agencies and did not involve the work permit holders themselves; a woman who failed to disclose she was pregnant when asked if she had any children; and children, coming to join families, who failed to disclose that their fathers had died a few months before they arrived.

The House of Lords decided to review the *Zamir* ruling after the unusually short period of two years. In the case of *Khera*, reported in *The Times* on 14 February 1983, it was held that the failure to reveal facts to an immigration officer would be grounds for removal only if the deception was intentional. Contradicting *Zamir*, the court decided that there was no positive duty of candour owed by an immigrant. The House of Lords also said that in deciding whether someone was an illegal entrant or not, the courts should enquire into the full facts and not merely accept the word of the Home Office. The *Khera* judgement is an important restriction on the law as it was stated in *Zamir*. However, the general expansion of the law which had taken place between 1973 and the *Zamir* judgement remains untouched.

Notwithstanding the *Khera* decision, it is evident that in collaboration with the Home Office, which itself pursued cases on the basis of an ever-widening definition of illegal entrant, the courts have extended the scope of the law beyond what was anticipated by most people when it came into force, and also have undermined the security of many people who thought they were permanently settled in the UK. Far from standing as a bulwark of freedom between the individual citizen and the excesses of the Home Office, they have chosen (with few exceptions) to side with the Home Office and have confirmed the view of the black presence in Britain as a presence unwanted.

## Judges and race: supporting racism

The courts' interpretation of the Race Relations Acts and their attitudes to the rights of black people have been scarcely less restrictive. Early cases showed a clearly restrictive attitude on the part of the higher courts.[3] In 1972, for example, the House of Lords heard the case of Stanislaw Zesko, a Polish national who had fled to Britain during the second world war and who had lived here since. In 1966 and again in 1968, Zesko applied to Ealing Borough Council to be placed on the housing waiting list. His applications were refused under a council rule which said that applicants had to be British nationals as defined by the British Nationality Act 1948. Zesko, backed by the Race Relations Board, alleged discrimination under the Race Relations Act 1968. This made it unlawful to discriminate on grounds of 'national origins'. The House of Lords ruled, by a majority of four to one, that there was no unlawful discrimination because 'national origins' did not mean 'nationality'. The Lords argued that parliament could have used the word 'nationality' if it had wanted. Its failure to do so meant that discrimination on grounds of nationality was intended to be exempt from the Act.

Professor John Griffith, in his study of the politics of the judiciary, comments that, even allowing for the conservatism of the House of Lords, this case showed a

> more than usually restrictive attitude. The alternative interpretation of the legislation was so clearly available to their Lordships that it is impossible to avoid the conclusion that theirs was a deliberate policy decision.[4]

A similarly restrictive attitude was adopted in 1973 when the House of Lords considered the case of a black man who had applied to join his local Conservative club. The county court rejected his complaint of discrimination but the Court of Appeal upheld it. The club appealed to the House of Lords and their appeal was upheld by a majority of four to one. The 1968 Act made it unlawful to discriminate in the provision of facilities or services to the public or 'any section of the public'. The Lords decided that club members were not a 'section of the public' and therefore they could be discriminated against. A similar decision was made in 1974, this time in relation to a dockers' club where a black visitor was told by the secretary, 'We do not serve coloured people.' The man was a member of another club and, as such, was an associate member of the dockers' club. Again the question was whether associate members were a 'section of the public' and therefore entitled to the protection of the Race Relations Act. The county court and the Court of Appeal said they were. The House of Lords, this time unanimously, said they were not and found in favour of the dockers' club.

John Griffith comments that it is difficult to believe that, in making their decision, the House of Lords did not consider the effect of their views on race relations. The different views taken by the Court of Appeal and the Lords can be explained by the different views taken of interpretation. The Court of Appeal took a more liberal view, interpreting the law in the spirit in which it was enacted. The House of Lords, however, took a conservative and restrictive view which regarded the law as an interference with the personal rights of those who wanted to discriminate and which had therefore to be interpreted as strictly as possible. The rights of black people were secondary.[5]

The different courts have adopted a similarly inconsistent but ultimately restrictive approach in their interpretation of the Race Relations Act 1976 and related legislation. Of particular importance has been the right of immigrants to public housing. In 1977, the Court of Appeal, Lord Denning presiding, held that two Italian families who had come to the UK were not entitled to housing under the Housing (Homeless Persons) Act 1977. The Act placed a duty on local authorities to give priority to those who were homeless, although they had no duty to those who had made themselves 'intentionally' homeless. The Court of Appeal ruled that by coming to Britain without ensuring they had permanent accommodation, the families had made themselves homeless intentionally. In fact, both families had lived with relatives and only sought council housing when asked to leave. As nationals of an EEC country they were also entitled under EEC law to enjoy all the rights and benefits given to national workers. The Court was not persuaded. Lord Denning stated:

> If any family from the Common Market can fly into Gatwick, stay a month or two with relatives and claim to be unintentionally homeless, it would be a most serious matter for the overcrowded borough. The borough should be able to do better than King Canute. He bade the rising tide at Southampton to come no further. It took no notice and he got his feet wet. I trust the councillors of Crawley will keep theirs dry against this new advancing tide.[6]

The Divisional Court, however, ruled in 1980 that a local authority *was* responsible for housing a refugee, even though she had no connection with the area. Mr Justice Griffiths said that he sympathised with the local authority, which argued that it could not have been the intention of parliament to make local councils liable to house all who came to Britain from abroad. But, he said, strict immigration control meant that 'all and sundry' did not arrive homeless. The decision was upheld by the Court of Appeal.[7]

In May 1981 the Court of Appeal, again with Lord Denning presiding, returned to the housing rights of homeless immigrants. In the case of *Islam*, the court held that a Bangladeshi man who had lived and worked in Britain since 1965 had made himself and his family intentionally homeless by bringing the family to Britain from Bangladesh without ensuring that he had permanent accommodation for them. Islam's home, Lord Denning said, was not in England but in Bangladesh where the family lived and where Islam 'occupied' a house with his wife and children. When they ceased to occupy it, he ceased to occupy it also. He was therefore intentionally homeless and not entitled to local authority priority housing. Lord Denning said that men from overseas should not bring wives and children to the UK unless they had arranged permanent occupation for them. This decision was overruled by the House of Lords in uncompromising terms. Lord Wilberforce said that the case fell 'four square' within the Housing (Homeless Persons) Act. Mr Islam was homeless, he was entitled to priority, he never had any 'available accommodation' which he could give up. There was, he concluded, 'no answer to his claim'.[8]

The courts have taken a generally restrictive view of the Race Relations Act, although there have been few cases. In 1980 the Home Office challenged the right of the Commission for Racial Equality (CRE) to carry out a formal investigation into the administration of immigration control. Under the 1976 Act the Commission has power to mount such investigations into suspected discrimination. The Home Office argued that it could never have been the intention of parliament that the CRE should have power to carry out an investigation of this kind. Peter Scott QC for the Home Office stated:

> The whole system of immigration control is based upon discrimination. It is of the essence of the Immigration Act that people will be discriminated against on the grounds of race or nationality and it is the function of certain officials to ensure that discrimination is effective.

Although the Divisional Court held that it was within the power of the CRE to carry out this investigation, Mr Justice Woolf reassured the Home Office saying that he thought it likely that the investigation would come to nothing since it required the cooperation of the Home Secretary in obtaining information. The consequences might not therefore be so drastic as the Home Office feared.[9]

The same judge stopped a proposed investigation by the CRE into the housing policies of Hillingdon Borough Council in the following year. The Commission had announced its intention to carry out an investigation after the chair of the council's housing committee refused to house a homeless Asian family but instead sent them to the Foreign Office claiming that it was their responsibility. Mr Justice Woolf said it was 'wholly unreasonable and vexatious' for the Commission to embark on a general investigation on the evidence available to it. He also thought that the investigation was too general and too wide-ranging. In August 1982, the House of Lords agreed and the investigation was scrapped.[10]

The decision which probably most angered Britain's black community was made by Lord Denning in September 1982. He ruled that Sikhs were not a racial group in the terms of the Race Relations Act 1976 and could therefore be discriminated against. The case concerned a boy who had been sent home from school because he wore a turban. The Court of Appeal ruled that this was not unlawful discrimination because Sikhs were a religious group, not an ethnic or racial one. As a result they fell outside the scope of the Act. The Court also severely criticised the CRE which had brought the case. Lord Justice Kerr said that, 'All that the commission has achieved in this case, as it seems to me, is to create racial discord where there was none before.'[11] This decision is contrary to the intention of parliament when passing the law. At the time, an amendment on religious discrimination was withdrawn when the government assured MPs that the new concept of indirect discrimination would cover unjustifiable discrimination against Sikhs.

The courts have matched their capacity for restrictive interpretation of immigration law with a similarly restrictive attitude to determining the rights of black people and immigrants living here. Favourable decisions do not affect this overall assessment. In the case of the refugee who was given housing there were strong compassionate grounds, but the court made it clear that strict immigration control ensured there would be few such cases. In the case of *Islam* it was absurd to say that the man's home was somewhere he had not lived for almost 20 years; and in the case of the CRE investigation into immigration control the judge thought the investigation could do little 'harm'.

It would be wrong to see the prejudices of individual magistrates as the sum of racism in the courts. The individual or collective racism of those who work in and run the courts is only one facet of a system that is based on racist principles and practice. However, the instances of racist attitudes are disturbing. In 1977, presiding over the trial of John Kingsley Read, chair of the British National Party, for incitement to racial hatred, Judge Neil McKinnon aroused considerable hostility and concern when he told Read on his acquittal, 'I wish you well.' Read had told a meeting: 'Fellow racialists, fellow Britons, and fellow Whites, I have been told I cannot refer to coloured immigrants. So you can forgive me if I refer to niggers, wogs and coons.' Then, referring to the murder of Gurdip Singh Chaggar in Southall the week before, Read said, 'Last week in Southall, one nigger stabbed another nigger. Very unfortunate. One down, a million to go.'

McKinnon directed the jury that the law against incitement to racial hatred did not cover 'reasoned argument in favour of immigration control or even repatriation'. He remarked to the jury,

> goodness knows, we have a million and a half or more unemployed already and that all the immigrants are going to do is to occupy the jobs that are needed by our local population. These are matters upon which people are entitled to hold and to declare strong views expressed in moderate terms . . . It is difficult to say what it is that this defendant is alleged to have done that amounts to a criminal offence.

McKinnon described Read as 'obviously a man who has had the guts to come forward in the past and stand up in public for the things he believes in.' Within ten minutes of McKinnon's summing up, the jury returned a verdict of not guilty. The judge told Read, 'You have been rightly acquitted but in these days and in these times it would be well if you were careful to use moderate language. By all means propagate the views you may have but try to avoid involving the sort of action which has been taken against you. I wish you well.' No formal action was taken against McKinnon. The Lord Chancellor, Lord Elwyn-Jones, accepted McKinnon's assurance that he had intended no offence to the immigrant community and that he in no way approved of Read's political aims. It was reported that McKinnon had asked the Lord Chancellor that in future he should not hear cases involving race; this request was granted.[12]

It would be wrong to see McKinnon as an isolated example of

racism and prejudice in the courts. He was perhaps an extreme example but there are numerous other instances of judges venting their prejudices in the safety of their courts. Judges and magistrates seem particularly prone to this when sentencing those who come before them. Colonel Ronald Laurence Gardner-Thorpe, the senior magistrate and alderman of the City of London, asked a black defendant who came before him for non-payment of a fine, 'Have you ever thought of going back to Barbados? I am a member of an organisation which would gladly pay your fare.'[13] Judge Gwyn Morris blamed immigrants for the decline of inner city areas. Sentencing five young blacks for robberies in 1975 he said,

> These attacks became a monotonous feature in the suburbs of Brixton and Clapham, areas which within memory were peaceful, safe and agreeable to live in. But the immigrant settlement which has occurred over the past 25 years has radically transformed that environment. Those concerned with maintenance of law and order are confronted with immense difficulties.[14]

Neil McElligott, magistrate at Marlborough Street, also sought to blame people from abroad for crime when he told a shoplifter from the Lebanon that 75 per cent of shoplifting cases involved people from her parts of the world 'who come to this country just to thieve'. Again no action was taken; indeed the Attorney General, Sir Peter Rawlinson, said in parliament that he thought the remarks were justifiable.[15]

Other judges have claimed for themselves some sort of understanding of the background and cultures of immigrants who come before them. At Middlesex Crown Court, Judge Solomon, sentencing a Jamaican for allowing himself to be driven in a stolen car, claimed that 'the tragedy of the West Indies is the lack of family life, as we understood it here in Britain.'[16] Judge Wild at Cambridge Crown Court a few days later told two Libyan students, 'This all came about because you got drunk and it is a pity that you did not have the decency to stand up and admit it. But then, as people about the courts know, people of your origin never admit anything, well, hardly anything.'[17] In Glasgow in

1981 Sheriff Francis Middleton, sentencing a white man for unlawful sexual intercourse with a 13-year-old Asian girl, said that under 'normal circumstances' he would have sent him to prison but he was only fining him because, 'Girls mature much earlier in the East. Until recently marriages were arranged at a very early age. In the form of marriage that takes place there, intercourse occurs before marriage. This may have predisposed her to this action.' The 'normal circumstances' implied the crime would have been greater if the girl had been white. The Secretary of State for Scotland declared himself satisfied that 'there was no racist element intended by Sheriff Middleton either in his sentence or his remarks.'[18] In October 1982, fining an Iranian £750 for theft of baby clothes worth only £2.50, a magistrate in Wells Street court claimed that the Shah's opposition to shoplifting had been one of the factors leading to his downfall. He said that the Shah had broadcast to the nation warning that Iranians convicted of shoplifting abroad would lose their passports. As a result of this and other factors, the magistrate said, he was deposed.[19]

## Prosecution policy

Time and time again the most serious of criminal charges have been brought against black defendants. This goes back at least to the first big Mangrove trial which ended in 1971. As a result of a demonstration against police harassment of the Mangrove, 27 people were arrested and charged variously with assault, possession of offensive weapons and obstruction of the police. Later, serious charges of incitement to riot and affray were brought against eight men and women. At committal proceedings, which are supposed to test the sufficiency of the prosecution case, the magistrate rejected the incitement charges. Undeterred, next day the prosecution brought new charges of riotous asembly. These charges were also rejected but the charges of affray were allowed to stand. The prosecution, however, did not give up and charges of riot were brought again when the cases came to the crown court. They were brought by means of a procedure that allowed for the circumvention of committal proceedings. This procedure involved what is known as a voluntary bill of indictment. This was prepared by the Director of Public Prosecutions against a ninth man who had not been arrested and charged with the others but had been arrested much later. He was charged with riot and affray at the Mangrove demonstration and the bill of indictment sought to bring him to trial with the other Mangrove defendants without committal proceedings. It did not mention that the committal proceedings for the eight had rejected riot charges. This, the trial judge said, was not a matter for him and the new charges were allowed to go ahead.

In the event, after a ten-week trial costing some £60,000, all nine defendants were acquitted of riot charges and only two were convicted of affray. They were given suspended prison sentences. Of the 32 charges brought, only nine stood. [20]

Undeterred by the result of the Mangrove trial, the prosecution brought serious charges of affray against more black defendants in the same year. Four of those arrested after a police raid on the Metro youth club in Notting Hill in May 1971 were charged with possession of offensive weapons and causing grievous bodily harm, and also with affray. [21] There were no convictions.

Affray charges were again brought against those arrested after a police raid on the Carib club in Cricklewood in 1974; 12 were charged with affray, malicious wounding, assaulting the police and causing grievous bodily harm. Nine were acquitted at the trial, one was acquitted after a re-trial and two were acquitted on appeal. [22] The prosecution authorities, however, seemed to have adopted the strategy if-at-first-you-don't-succeed . . . and following the policing of the bonfire night celebrations in Chapeltown, Leeds, in 1975 brought nine charges of affray. This time, the prosecution obtained three convictions, but overall there were 21 acquittals out of 24 charges relating to the events of bonfire night itself.

Following the Bristol disturbances in 1980, 16 people were selected from over 100 charged to face charges of riotous assembly. The charges, said one defence solicitor, were 'intensely speculative' but the Director of Public Prosecutions replied curtly that the decision to proceed with the charges had been made after 'lengthy consideration'. Despite this, charges against four defendants were dismissed by the magistrate at committal; three defendants were acquitted on the directions of the trial judge; and the jury acquitted five others. In four cases, the jury was unable to agree on a verdict and the charges were dropped. Shortly afterwards, the DPP agreed that it might have been a mistake to bring charges of riot.[23]

The serious charges brought against black defendants have not been limited to those of substantive public order offences. Equally important and equally severe have been the charges of conspiracy which have been brought on a number of occasions. Conspiracy charges have always been an important weapon of the state in dealing with critics and opponents. In several ways, it is more advantageous to the state to resort to charges of conspiracy than to use charges of specific offences. Conspiracy requires less proof than substantive charges, it can be used when no evidence of the actual offence has been obtained, and the parties to the alleged conspiracy need not even have met. Because it is generally an agreement between two or more people to do something it allows the prosecution to present in court all manner of evidence designed to show some relationship between the defendants, including evidence of political affiliations, beliefs and lifestyles. In addition, until the Criminal Law Act 1977, conspiracy charges carried more severe penalties than specific offences.

The first major conspiracy trial involving black defendants was that of *Kamara* in 1972 which followed the occupation by students from Sierra Leone of the High Commission in London. The students were convicted of unlawful assembly and conspiracy to trespass. They appealed on the grounds that the latter was not an offence known to English law. The case went as far as the House of Lords and the Lord Chancellor, Hailsham, delivered a judgement of considerable political importance. Conspiracy to commit any criminal act was, he said, a serious offence and an appropriate charge in the 'vast majority' of cases of occupations of premises. Conspiracy to trespass was a criminal offence where the 'domain of the public' was invaded. Such 'public domain' included embassies and the like. The decision, from the highest echelons of the legal establishment, gave conspiracy a definition wider than that previously accepted. One lawyer prophesied that it would have 'a chilling effect on political protest'.[24] The offence was abolished by the Criminal Law Act 1977 but replaced by a new specific offence of trespassing on embassy property.

Conspiracy charges were used against the Islington 18, youths arrested following the Notting Hill carnival in 1976 and charged with 90 offences of theft and robbery, including 30 charges of conspiracy to rob and commit theft. The vagueness of conspiracy charges was explained by the trial judge in his summing up: conspiracy was an agreement between two or more persons to commit an unlawful act and consisted of the agreement alone. The judge said that this agreement 'can be reached without words, over a cup of coffee or a can of Coke'. The trial ended in August 1977 after 15 weeks and the jury was out to consider its verdicts for 170 hours, then the longest period in the history of the Central Criminal Court. Despite all this, the jury convicted on only eight charges of theft and robbery. Three people were acquitted of all charges and all the conspiracy charges relating to the Carnival were dismissed. Not surprisingly, some court officials were heard to describe the proceedings, which cost £250,000 of public money, as 'a farce' and 'the biggest waste of time and money' ever seen at the Old Bailey.[25]

As with public order offences the police and the prosecution seemed undeterred and in 1978 proceeded with charges of conspiracy to rob against a further group of black youths in Lewisham, south London. This time, however, their case was supported by secretly taken video film which showed the activity of black youth at a particular bus stop, but not actual criminal activity. It was sufficient, however, to convince a jury who convicted all 19 youths.[26]

In the summer of 1981 12 black youths in Bradford were charged with conspiracy to damage property and endanger the lives of others and conspiracy to cause grievous bodily harm after they had made petrol bombs. In this case, however, there appeared to be substantial evidence that the 12 were involved together in which case the use of conspiracy charges by the prosecution appeared to be a way of ensuring that the youths were convicted, and that they received heavy sentences. Their case would therefore serve as a warning to others. The 12 accepted, however, that they had made the petrol bombs, that, in effect, they had 'conspired'. But, they argued, they had done so not for any criminal purpose but to defend themselves and their community from attack. They had exercised their right to self-defence, a right long recognised, at least in theory, by the law. The jury decided to accept their argument and all 12 were acquitted.[27]

## Bail and trial

The Bradford Twelve did not only have to face serious charges carrying a possibility of imprisonment for life. They were also remanded in prison for periods of up to three months before their trial. Eventually bail was granted with the strictest conditions. Sureties of up to £20,000 were required, passports had to be surrendered, a curfew from 10 p.m. to 7 a.m. was imposed, daily reporting to the police was required, and, in an effort to destroy the locally based and nationally supported defence committee, the defendants were banned from political activity and forbidden to meet one another except in the presence of a solicitor.

Strict conditions had also been imposed in the case of the Islington 18. By the time the cases came to trial six months after the arrests, eight of the defendants were still in prison. Others had been released only after intense police opposition on the grounds that witnesses would be intimidated, the youths would abscond and that they had previous convictions. (In one case this amounted to the theft of a sandwich four years previously.) One youth was required to find £3000 in sureties, all had to report to police daily (one, aged 14, had to report twice daily) and most had curfews imposed on them.

Such extreme examples are added to the many daily cases where the granting or refusal of bail is simply one more means by which the police, and by agreement the courts, impose their control over black people. The legal presumption in favour of bail does not even figure in their calculations.

Cases involving black defendants may be deliberately allocated to magistrates who are known for their 'touch' approach. A study of trials by academics Maureen Cain and Susan Sadigh in a south London court over a period of several weeks found that cases involving West Indian defendants were significantly more likely to be allocated to a 'tough' stipendiary magistrate than were cases involving white defendants. (The distinction made between 'tough' and 'soft' magistrates was one made by court workers themselves and referred to sentencing and attitudes.) Thus, 71.4 per cent of the cases involving West Indians went to the 'tough' magistrate, as did 55.6 per cent of cases involving other blacks, both higher proportions than the 45.9 per cent of cases involving white defendants. When it came to cases allocated to the 'soft' magistrate, only 4.8 per cent of the West Indian cases were allocated to him compared with 27.4 per cent of the white cases. The researchers concluded that the evidence was 'consistent with a racist practice on the part of the court administrators'. The magistrates themselves were not necessarily racist. There was some evidence that the 'tough' magistrate was 'tough' in all the cases he heard. One of the remarks noted by the researchers is typical of his approach; he told a black defendant, 'Whatever you do in your country I don't know, but you don't tell lies in this country, get that into your thick head. If you're going to live in England you're going to behave like an Englishman and tell the truth or you can leave.'[28]

Once cases actually get to court there is evidence of racism in the proceedings themselves. The unwillingness of most magistrates to disbelieve the evidence of police officers is widely known, and in its evidence to the Royal Commission on Criminal Procedure in 1979, the Institute of Race Relations cited a number of cases illustrating convictions reached on insufficient evidence. For example, one juvenile was arrested in the street for theft from a woman on the other side of the street. The woman refused to come to court saying she had seen nothing and that nothing had been stolen from her. Despite this the magistrates convicted. Four years later the same youth was arrested on a charge of attempted theft. The magistrate heard three different stories from three different police officers and on the basis of this convicted. Charges of 'sus' have also been upheld on the basis of slight evidence. For example, two youths were arrested at Oxford

Circus tube station and charged with 'sus'. A woman standing next to them told the police she had not seen the woman from whose handbag they were supposed to have tried to steal, and she denied that the behaviour of the youths had been suspicious. The magistrate interrupted the police officer giving this evidence, 'I hope you told her to get out of the way and mind her own business.' The officer replied that he had done so and the magistrate replied, 'Quite right. I don't approve of that kind of person.' The youths were convicted.[29]

## Special measures

In addition to such routine occurrences, in particular cases affecting the black community, special measures have been taken in the conduct of criminal proceedings. The experiences of the Southall trials of 1979–80, the Thornton Heath murder trial of 1981–82, the 1981 riots trials and the Bradford Twelve trial of 1981–82 all illustrate the extent to which the state is prepared to bend the rules of criminal procedure to achieve the results it desires.

The trials following the anti-fascist demonstrations in Southall on 23 April 1979 were not held in the nearby Ealing courts but were allocated to the magistrates' court at Barnet some 20 miles away. The 342 people charged as a result of the day's events had to make the long journey across London only to observe what one of the defence lawyers described as 'a striking and well-observed example of the subjectivity and inconsistency which permeates the magistrates court system'. Indeed, such was the conduct of the cases that 38 defence lawyers, in an unprecedented move, protested to Lord Hailsaham, the Lord Chancellor, of 'a magisterial bias against the defendants as a whole'. The number of arrests, the decision to remove the cases from people's home areas and the ability of magistrates to 'consistently and unconditionally accept the evidence of police officers in the face of credible defence evidence' combined, they said, to intimidate the Asian community. The Lord Chancellor rejected the accusations as 'so wholly improbable that I can only regard the suggestions as irresponsible'. The fact is, however, that following such protests the rate of convictions did decrease, giving credence to the protests. By then the damage had been done. As one defence lawyer put it, the court proceedings had come 'as the final blows in a sequence of affronts which began with the occupation of their Town Hall by racists on April 23rd . . . for the Southall community the lesson is that the courts were the final stage in a process of victimisation which began with the National Front.'[30]

On 1 June 1981 in Thornton Heath, south London, a teenager, Terry May, was pulled from his motorcycle and stabbed to death. A pub nearby was widely reputed to be used by National Front and British Movement activists and was attacked by black youths. Fifteen black youths were charged, some with May's murder and others with riot or affray. At committal proceedings defence lawyers attempted to explain the background and context of the murder and shed light on the racist history of the area where there had been vicious assaults on black people. The Attorney General stepped in to curtail the committal proceedings and have the case sent immediately for trial. He did this by means of a voluntary bill of indictment, the same procedure used in the Mangrove Nine trial. One of his reasons was that he was concerned about the 'racial lines of some of the defence questioning'. The Attorney General's application was granted having been heard in secret and in the absence of defence lawyers. Consequently, the case came to trial several months earlier than normal and the defendants were deprived of their right to test the prosecution case and apply for it to be dismissed for lack of evidence.

Proceedings had already started in the Bradford Twelve case where the central issues were white violence, police failure to deal with it and the right of the black community to defend itself. The date of the May trial was brought forward so that public attention was shifted to black violence. The Attorney General knew that the media would cover the trial fully and luridly, as had been the case with May's death itself. ('Innocent victim of race hate' said the *Daily Express*[31] which, like most other papers, devoted only a fraction of the space given to this case to the murder of a Pakistani, Mian Azum, the previous day.) The trial was used to deflect criticism of the police and government in their handling of racial violence, and yet again portrayed the black community as criminals.[32]

The riots of 1981 were inextricably linked to race and to black people and were widely regarded as 'race riots' by press, police and politicians. In fact they did not involve only black people. The trials that followed illustrate how the courts can behave in a situation of civil disturbance where race is perceived to be a major factor. It should be emphasised, however, that there is relatively little precise, documented information available about the trials and even less specifically about the treatment of black people. The following account is based on Home Office statistics and on material published by the Legal Action Group.[33]

Disregard for normal procedures was a hallmark of the criminal proceedings that followed the riots of April and July 1981. All over England, there were reports of hearings conducted with undue speed, remands in custody, stiff sentences, defence lawyers working under great pressure and courts' disregard for defence arguments and witnesses.

Almost all of those arrested (95 per cent) were also charged, the majority with public order offences such as riot, unlawful assembly, affray and obstruction of the police. Others faced charges of burglary, theft, handling of stolen goods, violence against the person or criminal damage. In general, the police appeared to have learned 'the lesson of Bristol' and brought summary charges, especially 'using threatening words or behaviour likely to cause a breach of the peace'. Defendants on such charges were not able to elect for trial by jury.

Bail was frequently denied to those arrested in the disorders. In Camberwell Green magistrates' court, which dealt with the Brixton cases, only 35 per cent of those making their first appearance in court after arrest received conditional bail, while only 17 per cent were given bail without conditions. One solicitor described what happened as 'a policy of internment' and another told of a magistrate who had remanded to prison a single woman with children, saying that he would not grant bail until the troubles died down. The solicitor took the woman from the prison van, made another bail application and was successful only because, as the magistrate put it, it was an 'exceptional circumstance'.

In Nottingham, under 16 per cent of those appearing in court after arrest were released on bail. Again, magistrates made it clear that they would grant bail only in exceptional circumstances. In one case a defendant was even denied an opportunity to ask for bail. In Leeds bail was granted to only 4 per cent of defendants making their first appearance, while in Liverpool, nearly 70 per cent were refused bail on their first appearance. One court remanded 22 out of 23 defendants in custody. A solicitor told of obtaining bail for only one client out of 26 he represented that day, while another told of a registered disabled man who had wanted to plead guilty to stealing a steak and kidney pie. He too was refused bail. In Manchester, 58 per cent of the defendants were granted bail, but the majority had conditions attached.

Where bail was granted, either on first appearance in court or later, conditions were frequently attached. Those bailed often had to provide sureties of £100 or £200 and many had to observe curfews, for example from 8 in the evening until 7 in the morning.

Three quarters of those who had been dealt with by July 1982 had been convicted. The overriding tendency, to judge from solicitors' accounts, was for courts to accept police evidence and reject defence cases, even where the latter were convincing. Particularly in the earlier cases, many of those convicted were sent to prison immediately, even where they had no previous convictions. Overall, however, 40 per cent of those convicted of more serious, indictable offences were given prison sentences, while only 20 per cent of those convicted of lesser, summary offences were sent to prison, the majority being fined. Those who were unemployed were more likely to be sent to prison than those who were in work, 46 per cent compared with 29 per cent. Those classified as 'West Indian/African' by the police were also more likely to be sent to prison than white people, 38 per cent compared with 34 per cent, although only 23 per cent of the Asians convicted were sent to prison.

## Juries

A crucial aspect of the Bradford Twelve trial was the composition of the jury. The original panel of 75 from which the jury was to be drawn included only six black people, and of these two could not speak English and were therefore disqualified, two had gone away and one had not replied. The judge refused to summon a new panel which would be more representative of the population of the area but did allow, after considerable pressure from the defence, a merger with another jury panel. After using their right to challenge potential jurors and have them excluded, the defence finally achieved a jury of seven white and five black people. This was only one of many cases where black defendants have had to argue and struggle for a multi-racial jury, using their right of challenge to redress imbalanced, all-white juries.

In 1969 black activist Michael X facing a drugs charge objected to the all-white jury but the court usher, when asked by the judge, could find only one black person in the court building waiting to be called as a juror.[34] A few months later, however, the same judge rejected defence objections to an all-white jury. The defence lawyer asked the court to take judicial notice that a substantial number of white people in Britain were biased against black people. The judge replied sharply, 'I would not take notice of that because I do not think it to be a fact.'[35]

In the same year, the Pakistani Immigrants Welfare Association in Bradford found that no Pakistanis were shown on the electoral roll as being eligible for jury service, even though there were an estimated 20,000 Pakistanis in Bradford. (Until 1972, jurors had generally to be householders. Thus most women and many men who were tenants or lodgers were excluded from jury service.) A complaint of racial discrimination was made to the Race Relations Board. Bradford City Council claimed that people had been excluded for reasons of language, because electoral forms had not been returned, and because of the difficulty in establishing the ownership of multi-occupied houses. At the time, Tory MP Tom Boardman attempted to justify this racist practice. He claimed that there were some on the electoral roll 'whose limited knowledge of our language, our customs and our character' did not equip them to decide on questions of guilt. 'I do not believe', he said, 'that those who have spent most of their lives in other countries, with different standards and attitudes are qualified after a short time here to decide.'[36]

In the 1971 Mangrove trial a defence application for an all-black jury was dismissed and some years later black barristers appealing for some black jurors to hear a case involving black defendants were told that there was no black juror available in the building. Nor would the judge agree to adjourn the case until a panel including black people could be gathered.[37] At the Bristol riot trial in 1981 only extensive use of the challenge succeeded in getting four blacks onto the jury. A survey of nine juries the previous week showed not a single black juror hearing a case.

The right to challenge and remove people who are about to be sworn in as jurors has been used for two reasons. Firstly to try to achieve a multi-racial jury and secondly to exclude those who may be prejudiced and hostile to black defendants. The Criminal Law Act of 1977 reduced the number of challenges without reason from seven to three. In theory there remains an un-restricted right to challenge for valid reasons. Actually finding out what jurors might think was altogether more difficult. During the Angry Brigade trial in 1972 the judge had allowed the defence considerable scope in questioning potential jurors about possible political bias against the defence. Questions allowed included what newspapers the jurors read and whether they were members of the Conservative Party. The practice upset senior members of the judiciary and only a few months later Lord Widgery, the Lord Chief Justice, issued a practice direction to the courts advising them that 'it is contrary to established prac-tice for jurors to be excused on more general grounds such as race, religion or political beliefs or occupation.' A few months after that jurors' occupations were removed from the jury list. The decision was taken by Lord Hailsham, the Lord Chancellor, who feared that defendants were using their knowledge of jurors' occupations to decide whether or not to make a challenge. The right to challenge he claimed was being 'abused' by the defence 'in cases with political overtones'. The decision was made with-out any discussion in parliament but after consultations with the Home Secretary, the Attorney General and a number of judges.

Judges have occasionally, however, put questions to jurors about their beliefs and prejudices. In 1980 at Croydon Crown

Court one man claimed he was prejudiced against black people, the police and the judiciary. He was excused. The judge agreed that 'the interests of justice would be better served if you were not on a jury.'[38] The following year at the trial of Newton Rose, a black man accused of murder, the judge advised potential jurors to disqualify themselves if they held strong views against black people or supported parties of the extreme right. He also advised those who supported the 'extreme left like the Socialist Workers Party or the Anti-Nazi League' similarly to say they did not wish to serve.[39] In the Bradford Twelve trial the judge asked the jury panel and the jurors finally selected a number of questions. These were: were they or any member of their immediate family associated with or sympathetic to any group which had expressed dislike or suspicion of non-white citizens; were they or members of their family members of the National Front, British Movement or Column 88; was any member of the immediate family a serving police officer; and had they or any member of their immediate family suffered loss of any kind during the disturbances in Leeds and Bradford.[40] Given previous cases and the Lord Chief Justice's practice direction of 1972, such questions, designed by the defence and put through a sympathetic judge, were in themselves a significant victory.

Juries, therefore, have been responsible for throwing out insufficiently proven charges in a number of cases against black people. These include the 1971 Mangrove trial, the Metro case of the same year, the Carib club trial of 1974, the Chapeltown bonfire trial of 1975, the Islington 18 trials of 1976, the Bristol trial of 1981 and the Bradford Twelve trial of 1982. Such cases, which have involved defeats for the police and prosecution, have been factors, along with the other major political trials of the 1970s and 1980s, in building up hostility to the jury system from judges, senior police officers and politicians. The results of this hostility have been to reduce the right to opt for jury trial, secret police checking on the background of jurors, and curtailment of the right to challenge. The events after the Bristol trial illustrate this process.

After the trial, right-wing MP Alan Clark claimed that the acquittals showed 'that black jurors, whether out of racial loyalty, fear of intimidation or a combination of both, are highly unlikely to convict accused black persons of offences connected with civil disturbance',[41] and only months later this theme was taken up by one of the country's most senior judges, Lord Denning, the Master of the Rolls. Speaking at the Lord Mayor of London's dinner for the judiciary, Lord Denning spoke of the 'abuse of the right of challenge' by the defence at Bristol which he claimed was used to get a jury 'of their own choice or at any rate a jury on which there would be disagreement by more than two', thus avoiding conviction. In his book *What Next in the Law?* published a year later, he launched into an attack on black jurors saying that the English were no longer

> a homogeneous race. They are white and black, coloured and brown . . . some of them come from countries where bribery and graft are accepted . . . and where stealing is a virtue so long as you are not found out. They no longer share the same code of morals or religious beliefs.

Citing (with a number of inaccuracies) Bristol as an example of jury packing, Denning set out to show that not all British citizens were qualified to sit as jurors and that 'black, coloured and brown people do not have the same standards of conduct as whites'. After threats of legal action by two of the black Bristol jurors the book was hastily withdrawn and the offending passages removed. In addition, Denning, then 83, announced his retirement.

Leaving aside for the moment the outright racism of such 'arguments', what Denning and others choose to ignore is that it is the very randomness of the present jury system that results in all-white juries which do not reflect the multi-racial nature of society and the challenge has been used to redress this imbalance and to try to weed out those hostile to black people.

There have, of course, been cases where juries (even multi-racial ones) have returned verdicts against black people where the opposite verdict might have been expected, but it is worth noting that in three important such cases there were other factors at work. In the acquittal of John Kingsley Read of incitement to racial hatred, the judge at first discharged the jury after an extremely short period of consideration (two hours) and in the subsequent retrial leaned heavily towards Read's acquittal. In the Lewisham 21 case, where black youths were convicted of conspiracy to rob, secretly made video vilm, which showed no criminal activity but only the activity of some youths at a bus stop, nevertheless was the major piece of police evidence. As the Institute of Race Relations pointed out to the Royal Commission on Criminal Procedure: 'Such a method, invested with the apparent impartiality of a scientific exercise, lent substance and authority to the prosecution case; the film helped create a presumption of the youths' guilt within the court, implying that they must have taken part in a serious crime to have warranted such methods in the first place.'[42] More recently, in the trial of Newton Rose in 1981 for the murder of a white man, the trial judge, Edward Clarke, gave the jury a secret ultimatum at 5.45 p.m. that they had 15 minutes to reach a verdict or else they would be discharged and the whole case would have to be retried. At 6 p.m. the jury returned a verdict of guilty and Rose was sent to prison for life. The House of Lords eventually ruled that there had been a 'material irregularity' and crushed Rose's conviction.[43]

## Sentencing

There has been little systematic study of variations in the sentencing of black and white defendants. The courts themselves stand in a strong position to control or prevent such research. In 1976, for example, the community relations council in Wandsworth sought access to the records of the local magistrates' court which, it said, had become a 'centre of alarm over the punishment it has meted out, particularly to young blacks'. This access was simply refused by the chief magistrate.

In 1982 an article was published by two established and respected criminological researchers, Michael McConville and John Baldwin, which claimed that there was no evidence of direct, systematic bias on racial lines in crown court sentencing.[44] As the first systematic attempt in Britain to examine whether race was a factor in sentencing this research was particularly important. *The Times* headlined its report 'Blacks get a fair deal in court'. The research was, however, far from being the systematic study it purported to be. First, the figures used had in fact been gathered for other purposes and previous studies and some of them were several years old. Second, the study dealt only with crown courts and not magistrates' courts which deal with most criminal business. Third, the study did not establish whether race had any influence on the various criteria – previous criminal record, seriousness of offence – used to determine the level of sentencing. As black people are more likely to be arrested for some offences, they are more likley to have a criminal record. The study, therefore, did not establish that race was irrelevant in sentencing.[45] In particular, it simply failed to explain the evidence that blacks were disproportionately represented in the prison population.

For some time there has been considerable evidence that a larger number of black people were being sent to prison than one would expect from their numbers in the population at large. When Terence and Pauline Morris were writing their classic study of Pentonville Prison in the early 1960s they found that 4.4 per cent of the prisoners were black. At the time this was approximately proportional to the black population of Greater London. By 1970, however, the proportion of black prisoners in the prison had risen to between 8 and 10 per cent. In 1973 a recently released prisoner told *Black Voice* that the black population in prisons appeared to be between 15 and 20 per cent and an estimate of the black borstal population in 1976 was given by the Home Office as just under 10 per cent. By 1981 the National Prisoners' Movement, PROP, was claiming from reliable sources inside the Home Office that the overall proportion of black prisoners was 17 per cent while for young prisoners it was more than double at 36 per cent. Finally the Home Office was compelled to say something and in 1982, for the first time, the Director General of the Prison Department made available some official figures. The black population of Ashford Remand Centre, he said, was 50 per cent, in Rochester, Blantyre and Dover young offenders institutions it was 30 per cent and in the three dispersal prisons in the south east it was 15 per cent. At around the same time the Prison Department announced that it was to start collecting information on the ethnic origins of all prisoners. This was not, however, the start of an attempt to investigate sentencing practices but the first step towards a policy of dispersal of black people in the prison system (see chapter 6).

A study of black people in borstal between 1974 and 1976, eventually published by the Home Office in 1981, found that on average black borstal trainees had fewer previous convictions than their white counterparts. The author Neil Fludger wrote, 'they have arrived in borstal at an earlier stage in their criminal careers.' This might be explained by a higher proportion of violent offences by black trainees but Fludger studied this and found that it could not be the explanation, though he declined to say what might be.[46]

Part, at least, of the explanation is that magistrates are more likely to imprison young offenders and others if they are jobless, homeless or have been in care. A study of unemployment, crime and imprisonment showed that the unemployed were more likely to be sent to prison than those with jobs. The point was explained by black solicitor Paul Boateng who said that, 'One of the most important factors in any plea of mitigation is the client's employment status . . . In borderline cases it can be the deciding factor.'[47] If this is so, and there is no reason to doubt it, then black people in trouble and particularly young black people in trouble are especially likely to end up in prison given that unemployment among black people is consistently far higher than it is among whites. One result of racism – in employment – in turn leads to another – in the courts.

If black people are more likely than whites to end up in prison, then they are also less likely to be given probation. A study of the West Midlands, the second largest probation area in the country, found that black people were significantly less likely that whites to be given probation orders under supervision but were more likely to be on probation after release from custody or under the Children and Young Persons Act 1969.[48]

The author of the study declined to offer any explanation for the differences but in another much smaller study it was shown that a majority of the probation officers questioned had stereotyped views of some black people, especially Rastafarians. Thus, over half the officers interviewed saw Rastas as having some sort of 'identity crisis', or they explained it as a 'rebellion against an authoritarian father figure', while others attributed it to the rejection of the work ethic and saw it as a result of the 'matriarchal structure of the West Indian family' and the 'absence of a strong father figure in primary socialisation'! Three probation officers did see Rastafarianism as a reaction to social inequality but they were unwilling to attribute these inequalities to discrimination, while only two of those interviewed described Rastafarianism as a response to racism. Not surprisingly, given these views, when 15 social enquiry reports were examined in only one case was there a recommendation by the probation officer for probation.[49] A combination of such discrimination in probation and in sentencing policy resulted, one professor of social administration estimated, in black people being three times as likely as whites to be given a custodial sentence.[50]

In addition to being sent to prison, some black people are also liable to find themselves being thrown out of the country altogether. Successive immigration laws not only prevented black people from coming to settle in Britain but also made more people liable to deportation. Under the present law any criminal court can make a recommendation to the Home Secretary that a non-patrial who has been convicted of any imprisonable offence (that is almost any offence) be deported. Such a recommendation is additional to any other sentence that may be passed. The courts have a wide discretion to make recommendations and people can be, and are, deported for trivial offences including shoplifting. A senior Queens Counsel has described the courts, especially the magistrates' courts, as 'perfunctory in the extreme' in recommending deportation.[51] In 1973, the courts made over 600 recommendations for deportation but by 1980 this had risen to 1242 recommendations. In 1981 the figure fell to 820. Not all recommendations for deportation are followed by the Home Secretary but the number of orders made after court recommendations is still high. In 1980 there were just over 800 such orders made and in 1981 just over 700. (The figures are not directly comparable as orders may relate to recommendations made in a previous year.) Even where no recommendation is made by a court the Home Secretary can still order deportation on the grounds that this is conducive to the public good and the Home Office requires the police to submit reports on people who are convicted and who are liable to deportation. The success rate in appeals against deportations is only 4 or 5 per cent. Since the Immigration Act 1971 came into force, 473 people have been deported under the Home Secretary's own powers while a further 4098 have been deported after court recommendations.[52]

Before they had the power to recommend the deportation of Commonwealth citizens, the courts had given themselves the power of what one lawyer has called 'quasi-deportation'. This meant that the courts used their common law power to bind over a defendant and attach as a condition that they leave the country. There were numerous such cases involving Irish defendants who were bound over to return to the Republic for various periods and in 1958 a court bound over a Nigerian, James Ayu, to return to Nigeria for five years. The binding over order was quashed on appeal but only because it had been imposed in addition to a prison sentence – not because there was anything wrong with it in principle. Lord Parker, the Lord Chief Justice, underlined this when he said, 'I should add that this case shows very clearly the need, which has already been canvassed, I understand, in other quarters, for there being a power to deport a man such as this.'[53] Four years later parliament took Parker's advice and extended the power of deportation to cover certain Commonwealth citizens. This did not end the practice of 'quasi-deportation' however and the most notorious of the cases involving a bind over to leave the country occurred in 1982, in a case arising from the 1981 riots. Carl Williams, an 18-year-old black youth who had been born in Britain was convicted of theft. As a patrial he could not be deported so instead he was bound over by the court on condition that he left the country for five years. (The judge had heard that the family planned to visit Jamaica to prepare to return to live there.) Williams accepted the condition only because he would otherwise have been sent to Borstal. The sentence, described by the National Council for Civil Liberties as 'repatriation by the back door', was quashed on appeal but the Court of Appeal affirmed that courts had the power to banish offenders but said that this should be used 'very sparingly'. It should be done 'very seldom' if the defendant did not freely consent but the fact that Williams had consented under threat of imprisonment did not of itself make such consent invalid. Nor did the Court of Appeal rule that courts should not send offenders to countries with which they had little connection. They could do this in 'exceptional circumstances'.[54]

Binding over without banishment has also been used to deal with black defendants. Tony Soares, the black activist charged with various serious offences after reprinting an article on making molotov cocktails, was sentenced to 200 hours of community service – a relatively lenient sentence – but was bound over for seven years. This was an attempt to curtail future political activity.

But one did not have to be convicted of a criminal offence in order to be bound over. Three black youths, who were acquitted by Marlborough Street magistrates' court of loitering with intent to steal, were banned from the West End for one year and bound over for £30. Magistrate Neil McElligott told them, 'There are too many people in this area coming before the court for this sort of thing.'[55]

Nor did one have to be facing criminal charges to be bound over, as magistrate Brian Canham showed during the Southall trials in 1979. Canham bound over defence *witnesses* for £100 to keep the peace. In one case involving an Asian man, Canham justified his action on the grounds of the man 'being in a hostile crowd and coming to court to excuse such behaviour.'[56]

That the liberal notion of the courts and the legal system as impartial and a bulwark between the state and the citizen is a myth is highlighted by the experience of the black community. Judges have undermined the security of that community through their interpretations of immigration law and, in particular, their widening definition of illegal entry. The most serious charges have been brought against black people and it is only with struggle that black people have obtained trials by their peers. This, in turn, has influenced moves to limit trial by jury. At the end of the legal process black people are more likely than whites to be sent to prison.

The courts have therefore continued and sanctioned the process whereby black people are defined by the state as a problem. Like the police, they have played their own part in the criminalisation, control and disciplining of the black community.

# 6. Prison racism

One cannot deny that the presence of the ethnic minorities in our prisons occasionally poses problems.
Home Office minister Patrick Mayhew, 1981[1]

Some days the vans arrive from the courts and you look at them, and you realise, Christ, they're *all* black.
Prison officer at Wandsworth, 1982[2]

The process of criminalisation which begins with the police and moves through the courts ends for increasing numbers of black people in prison or borstal. In April 1981 the prison population in England and Wales had risen to 44,000, the highest per population of any country in Western Europe. After the summer's riots, it had risen further to 45,500. This, according to the Director General of the Prison Department, imposed 'intolerable strains on local prisons and remand centres' and, even with the opening of emergency prison camps, 'The Prison Service continued for several weeks to operate at the margin of its ability to cope.'

## Black solidarity, white hostility

An increasing and disproportionately high number of black people are being sent to prison. The Home Office's decision to classify all prisoners' ethnic origins was not made as a result of official concern that black people might be the victims of discrimination in sentencing. In the words of the Prison Department, it was 'an attempt to prevent the development of serious racial problems'.[3] These 'racial problems' were not defined but it is clear that the presence of black prisoners has presented the Prison Department with two problems – neither *caused* by black prisoners. On the one hand there was increasing evidence of solidarity among black prisoners; on the other there was increasing evidence of racial hostility towards them. Both presented problems of control for the prison authorities.

Black prisoners had played an important part in the major prison demonstrations of the 1970s, for example, Hull in 1976 and Gartree in 1978. Accounts from prisoners at Hull published by PROP, the National Prisoners' Movement, in 1976, showed that there were a number of prison officers who were National Front members or sympathisers and that the black and Irish prisoners suffered most once the prison officers regained control. One claimed that he heard a black prisoner in the cell below being beaten up and cries of 'This is what we do to niggers' and 'National Front rule, OK nigger'.[4] Similar stories were repeated by prisoners at the subsequent trial of prison officers in 1979. One black prisoner told how he had been kept awake by officers switching his cell light on and off, kicking his door and shouting: 'National Front rules, big black bastard'. After being beaten, this prisoner had his breakfast thrown over him and was made to run a gauntlet of prison officers, 'to see if you can run like the other black athletes'. Once in his cell, the contents of a chamber pot were poured over him.[5]

At Gartree in 1978, black prisoners were among those who took over three wings of the prison in protest at the drugging of a black prisoner, Michael Blake. In the same year black prisoners played a key role in the demonstration over conditions at Wormwood Scrubs. On the third anniversary of the Hull riot, a peaceful demonstration of some 200 prisoners was brutally broken up by the prison MUFTI (Minimum Use of Force–Tactical Intervention) squad, a specially trained body of prison officers armed with staves and riot shields whose existence had never been formally, publicly acknowledged. The Home Office denied that any injuries had resulted from the break-up of the demonstration but was forced by the National Prisoners' Movement, PROP, to admit that 53 people had been injured. A prison visitor who earlier had described the injuries to prisoners was banned by the authorities.

In the subsequent report on the disturbance, finally published in 1982, the Regional Director of the South East Region of the Prison Department sought to blame the black prisoners in the Scrubs, at least in part, for what had happened. They were, he said, along with the London gangster prisoners and the IRA prisoners, one of a number of 'rival factions' which vied for power in D wing of the prison. Together, the three groups had been 'instrumental in creating an atmosphere of unrest and instability in which prisoners were encouraged to challenge the authority of management and staff' and generally they had exploited widespread dissatisfactions with the conditions in D wing.[6]

There is some evidence to suggest that individually black inmates were seen as no different from others, but that as a group they were seen by prison staff as troublesome. David Wickham, writing a thesis on black borstal boys at Rochester, found that group cohesiveness and solidarity seemed to constitute a threat to the system and the staff and that staff reacted on their own assumptions based on prejudiced and inaccurate ideas. He concluded that both staff and the black borstal trainees might have been exposed to an 'amplification process' which 'effectively turned a relatively innocuous, ordinary and conforming group of trainees into an allegedly difficult and notorious sub-group'. Therefore, in the eyes of the prison authorities, black prisoners were a bad influence on other prisoners and a threat to control in themselves.

An additional problem of control was presented in the racism inside prisons. The Prison Department had begun to maintain a register of 'racial incidents' in 1972 and recorded about five or six such incidents each year. Most of these involved only a few prisoners, but in 1977 the Home Office revealed that several months previously there had been serious fighting at Wormwood Scrubs between black and white prisoners in which some 30 people had been involved. A study of Rochester borstal quoted a memorandum from an assistant governor to the governor that, 'Twenty-eight per cent of the wing are non-white trainees and it is becoming increasingly difficult to maintain a peaceful equilibrium between them and the rest of the wing population. The situation is further exacerbated by the presence of highly prejudiced trainees.' That there was hostility to black prisoners was also accepted by the Regional Director's report into Wormwood Scrubs quoted above. He noted that while the development of black prisoners as a cohesive political group had some connection with the growth of black political consciousness over the last decade or so, 'in the prison environment it has more to do with self-protection and an attempt to secure a degree of institutional power'.

The prison authorities' response to such racist hostility was not to try to deal with it in accordance with the Director General's statement that, 'the objective of the prison service is that relations between different ethnic groups within establishments will remain harmonious.' Instead they took the same road as the government in relation to immigration. The problem became a problem of numbers. If there were fewer black prisoners there would be fewer problems. The difference was that the prison authorities could not keep people out of prison. The question was therefore one of dispersing the black prison population. Roshan Horabin, doing research for the Howard League for Penal Reform and the Runnymede Trust, had been told by prison staff in 1978 that problems of control and 'friction' arose when the black population went over one-third of the prison population and in 1981 the Prison Department, which had just announced its intention to classify ethnic origins, was said to be anxious not to let the black population get above 30 per cent in any one institution.[7]

So the prison authorities, in the pursuit of their primary aims of containment and control of prisoners, have ignored racism within prisons. Indeed there is some evidence from ex-prisoners to show that such racism was actually used by prison staff in the control of black prisoners, and that black prisoners were often made to share cells with known racists. The prison authorities have also chosen to ignore evidence of fascist support and racist activity among prison staff themselves.

## Racist prison staff

Allegations of fascism and racism among prison staff are not new. When Tom Clayton spent some time at Pentonville Prison in 1970 researching his book, *Men in Prison*, he judged that 'when Enoch Powell made one of his intemperate speeches on immigration he had no more fervent supporters than on the Pentonville landings'.[8] Such statements support the claims made by groups like the National Front which boast of the high number of prison officers who are either supporters or members. In 1976 Brian Baldwin, a prison officer at Strangeways Prison in Manchester for 14 years, claimed that there was a membership of more than 70 out of a staff of 300. He said

> It's not been hard to recruit them. They almost recruit themselves. The National Front has a particular appeal for prison officers. It is the only party which has made law and order a prime plank in its platform. And it says publicly what many of them say privately about other things, like too many immigrants and their hangers-on getting here and staying.[9]

Similar claims were made by a member of the NF Directorate and Lancashire organiser, Martin Goucher. He said that the strongest branches were at Walton Prison, Liverpool, Risley Remand Centre, Strangeways and Wandsworth where he claimed a membership of 15 to 20 per cent.[10] Ex-prisoners confirmed that officers had been told not to wear NF badges with their uniforms but wore instead Union Jack tie pins. One prison officer at Strangeways, although denying the claim that there were anything like 70 NF members or supporters among the staff, did admit that the acknowledged handful did 'get out of hand'.[11]

The prison authorities' response was to do nothing. The Governor of Strangeways denied that there was a NF group at the prison. He told the press:

> As far as individual membership of the National Front or Column 88 is concerned under Civil Service regulations some officers, among them prison officers, are free to belong to any

political organisation, except the IRA which is proscribed. If, however, allegiances to any such organisations interfered with the duties of a prison officer, and his political beliefs interfered with his duties, stern action would be taken.[12]

Merlyn Rees, the Home Secretary, was scarcely more encouraging. He told parliament that the NF was not a proscribed organisation and there were no grounds for not employing people who were members or supporters or for placing restrictions on them because of it. It was another matter if political views reflected attitudes to prisoners.[13] He subsequently rejected demands for an inquiry into the claims, saying that there was no evidence, and ignored the advice of one MP who told him that the only way to get the evidence was actively to seek it out.

The evidence continued to trickle out nevertheless. In 1977, the year after Rees's statement, a prison visitor at Pentonville spotted five officers from the prison taking part in a National Front march, and in the same year the Church of England chaplain at Brixton prison, Terry Spong (who once said he was 'proud to be white and British') resigned after the press reported on his boasting of his NF membership at the NF annual conference. In 1978, the anti-fascist magazine *Searchlight*, which has continually exposed fascism in British prisons, reported that the National Front had established a group in Princetown, near Dartmoor Prison, and had claimed that the majority of the members were prison officers. In an interview with the local paper, Brian Benwell, the chair of the Princetown Prison Officers' Association, said, 'Yes, there are members. I do know some members. Without telling you if I am a member of the National Front, I can assure you that I have had knowledge of the National Front since their beginning and I personally agree with a lot of their policies.'[14]

In 1980 John Merritt of the *Western Independent* examined allegations of attacks on prisoners in Dartmoor, a high proportion of which appeared to be racially motivated. In the course of his investigation he interviewed John Tyndall, then chair of the National Front, about NF activity in the prison service. Tyndall told him:

We do have a larger than average number of supporters of the National Front among prison officers. We are particularly strong at Strangeways, Pentonville and the Scrubs. Where prisoners are concerned it is also a fact that there are a higher proportion of coloureds than in most other places. The relationship between crime and race is obvious . . . It is possible that coloureds give them more aggravation in prison though. And therefore they provoke officers more, it is a fact that coloureds are more violently inclined. If a black inmate gave prison officers some aggravation and they responded by giving him a bit of a bad time then we would say fair enough, but we do try to weed out the more violent element.[15]

The following year, recently released prisoners from Wandsworth claimed that a number of prison officers were wearing Union Jack badges. Estimates were made of one in three showing such support for the National Front, while in the reception area through which all new prisoners pass, the number was three out of four. Again the response of those involved in the prisons was complacent. The Deputy General Secretary of the Prison Officers' Association, Peter Rushworth, said:

If it's being said that some of our members are National Front members, then our answer is it's possible, given that they are drawn from a broad cross-section of society. But the Prison Officers' Association is not politically affiliated and matters of religion and politics are members' own affairs.[16]

The same year there were reports that a racist leaflet, 'Nigger application for employment', was being given to black prisoners by prison officers at Strangeways and Wyemot near Leyland, although, not surprisingly, this was denied by the governors concerned. The leaflet, obviously US in origin, said no photo was required 'since you all look alike' and asked what machines the 'applicant' could operate, 'crowbar, pinball, gun, straight razor'; what foods were liked, 'Coon, Paki'; and asked 'applicants' to list 'your greatest desire in life – other than a white girl'.[17]

The official attitude towards members of fascist groups working in the prison service is that prison officers can belong to any organisation so long as they do not carry out their political activity in the prison and their political beliefs do not interfere with their duties. On the face of it, it would seem obvious that any member or supporter of a racist organisation which openly advocates the compulsory repatriation of the black population and whose leaders have been convicted for racial violence and incitement would not be able to carry out their duties impartially. The failure of the Home Office to take any action on the numerous allegations made indicates either that it fears the possible reaction of the Prison Officers' Association if officers were to be disciplined, or that it regards such allegations as something less than serious.

Ex-prisoners have claimed that in prisons where support for the NF is strong, black prisoners were frequently assaulted or abused. In Strangeways, several prisoners had stickers put on their doors saying 'Niggers Beware'; in Dartmoor golliwog stickers appeared on the doors of black prisoners' cells. One black prisoner graphically described what it was like to be in a prison where there was a number of National Front officers:

> From the time I was placed in the main prison I was a constant target for assault, abuse and harassment. My life became so bad that I suffered a nervous breakdown . . . There is a ritual in Manchester where all the black prisoners are forced to go down a walkway which is bordered by white lines. If you walk on the white line you are immediately clubbed down by the surrounding National Front members. The next stage of this set-up is when you are taken to a room, where you are ordered to strip off and bend down so they can all look up your arse, one by one, then pass comments and laugh in your face. I was to go through this many times, you were at their mercy and there was nothing you could do. The National Front run the prison and if you hit back when kicked you are liable to get your hand broken. This happened to one black prisoner and nothing was done about it.[18]

Other prisoners have said that the black prisoners were given the dirty jobs or the most badly paid, such as sewing or repairing mailbags or packing polythene bags. Prisoners released from Wandsworth in 1981 made allegations of violence towards black prisoners but said that far more common were 'niggly little things like "get your hands out of your pockets" or "button up your uniform".'[19]

Such behaviour contrasts sharply with behaviour towards known fascist prisoners. Derek Merry, a former National Front organiser in the West Country, claimed that the Front had sent information packs and stickers into Dartmoor Prison, 'but it's not just officers. We got a letter from a prisoner asking us to give him membership too. I'm not going to tell you how we got the stuff inside the prison.'[20] Even worse, a convicted racist murderer, Brian Hosie, serving life imprisonment in Peterhead Prison in the north of Scotland, was allowed to receive nazi literature and to correspond freely with known fascists. Hosie was convicted of murdering a West Indian in 1975. He told the police at the time that his action was 'an over-enthusiastic programme of repatriating our Commonwealth citizens' and said that his policy was to 'boost emigration, start extermination'. At the time he was a member of the National Front. In 1982 *Searchlight* revealed that Hosie was allowed to subscribe to the *League Review*, the journal of the fascist League of St George, and was allowed to send uncensored letters to officials of the League and other known fascists.[21] In the same year it became known that another prisoner in Peterhead was refused a copy of *Labour Weekly* because it contained an article about the prison, while another had been refused copies of the left-wing paper, *Fight Racism, Fight Imperialism*.

Only a few months later, Joe Pearce, former editor of the Young National Front paper *Bulldog*, emerged from a prison sentence for incitement to racial hatred, claiming that he had met support from staff at Chelmsford Prison. Right from the first day, Pearce claimed,

> it was made clear to me by the prison officers that they did not consider me to be a criminal or even that I had committed a criminal offence in their eyes. A number of officers boasted to me of their NF membership and several others enquired as to how they could get hold of NF publications.[22]

Racism in prisons is not, however, caused by fascist supporters or sympathisers in prison. This point has been well put by Geoff Coggan of PROP. Writing in *Searchlight* in November 1981 he said, 'If every National Fronter were to be dismissed tomorrow the racism would continue unabated. It is much more a matter of an inherently racist and brutal system attracting to their staff the creatures most suitable for carrying out these tasks.'

There is considerable evidence to support such a statement and to show that racism in prisons is not confined to members or even sympathisers of fascist organisations. In 1968 three Black Power activists on remand in Brixton alleged ill-treatment. A statement by the Black Peoples' Alliance to the Home Office complained that the men faced 'almost daily the most vulgar and provocative abuses and insults . . . they have been treated with physical violence . . . several times they have been either denied the normal prison right of having visitors or have their visiting time drastically shortened.'[23] In the same year Roderick Chambers, a black prisoner in Pentonville, was severely scalded in the bath house in an incident with another prisoner who had demanded his plug and brush. Chambers was so badly injured that he lost the use of his left arm and could walk only with difficulty. He was refused legal aid to sue the prison authorities for negligence in their standards of care and his application to the Criminal Injuries Compensation Board was also turned down. The Board said it was 'far from satisfied that the injuries were directly attributable to a criminal offence.'[24] A black prisoner wrote to *Race Today* in 1971 about conditions for black prisoners in an unnamed prison, saying that black prisoners were never allowed to 'bunch' at exercise and were allocated so that there were never two black prisoners in a cell. They quoted the governor telling one black prisoner, 'You people infest the country, demanding Black Power and God knows what, but I'll have none of your equality nonsense here.' The officers, he said, took their cue from the senior staff and the white prisoners followed the officers. 'Life for the black prisoner becomes a series of taunts, insults and humiliations.'[25] One black prisoner, Vernon Jones, a US seaman remanded to Barlinnie Prison in Glasgow after a disturbance near a US base on the Clyde, spent three months in solitary confinement before the trial and had the light kept on 24 hours a day. All this was apparently at the request of the state authorities of Alabama from where Jones originally came.[26]

Ron Philips was one of three black men in a batch of about 26 admitted to Strangeways. As he wrote: 'None of the three were left in any doubt as to where they were to stand in the prison's hierarchy.'

'Name!' bawled the reception officer.

'Gordon James.'

'Gordon James, what?'

'Gordon James, man, just Gordon James.'

'Not just Gordon James you stupid black twat! Gordon James, Sir!'

'Gordon James sir.'

'What religion James?'

'Church of God.'

'Church of God? What the fucking hell's that?'

'Well sir, it's . . .'

'Don't tell me what it is! I don't want to know what it is! You've got no religion! You're a fucking Moss Side ponce! That's your fucking religion . . . We got hundreds of you bastards in here . . . every one a fucking ponce! It's a fucking religion with you blokes. If I had my way, I wouldn't nick you, I'd fucking well top the lot of you! While you're here you'll be Church of England and like it! Empty your pockets!'[27]

Even outside researchers were to witness such attitudes. Roshan Horabin, carrying out research for the Runnymede Trust and the Howard League, was asked at one prison whether she had 'come to view the wogs?'. More subtly, racist statements were made by various prison staff in a series of articles which appeared in the *Guardian* in early 1982. The Governor of Aylesbury Prison claimed that 'When two blacks meet, it is a social event, and they can pose a threat just by moving slowly, gesticulating more, making more noise, talking in patois.' The prison's senior officer stated, 'their biggest problem is doing what they're told. They want to do everything at their own pace, which is generally slower than the rest, and they object to being hurried up.' An officer at Wandsworth complained that, 'They can be a nuisance in the reception block, going in or out, because they hold things up, washing at great length, oiling their faces.'[28] (This complaint of excessive hygiene is an interesting departure from the usual racist stereotype of the 'they-don't-wash-and-they-smell' variety.) An officer at Dover Borstal told of how black inmates could make themselves unpopular by 'playing reggae music loud and long, talking in West Indian dialect, playing dominoes with speed and fervour', and went on to talk of 'black racists' who could get almost total support from black inmates through 'sub-cultural pressures'.[29]

The routine racism of the prison service forced the prison authorities to act, albeit in a very limited way. In a memorandum in 1982, the Prison Department of the Home Office reminded all prison governors of the need for 'vigilance in ensuring that inappropriate racial comments were excluded' from reports submitted by prison staff to the Parole Board. It cited examples of what it called 'offensive and objectionable' remarks including 'typical young prisoner and black boy to boot', 'a devious character, typical of his race', and 'all the Asian traits, all smiles, eager to please and as dishonest as possible when opportunity presents itself'. The memorandum also noted the use of references to colour when this was irrelevant. It noted that, 'epithets like "arrogant coloured man" or "surly coloured man" imply a connection in the writer's mind between coloured people and arrogance or surliness, and this impression undermines any confidence in the reporting officer's judgment or objectivity'.[30]

But for some black people, the experience of prison proved too much. Horace Bailey, aged 23, on remand for three months for obstructing the police, an offence for which he would most probably have been fined if convicted, hanged himself in Ashford Remand Centre in 1973. Dennis Mulling hanged himself in Winson Green in 1974 while in prison for the first time. Earlier, two probation officers had informed prison medical staff that they feared he might attempt suicide. The senior medical officer told the coroner's inquest that he had decided that the situation did not require 'absolutely immediate attention' although he accepted that in the light of events he could have taken more action.[31]

More recently, in 1982, Paul Worrell, again on remand in Brixton, hanged himself with his own shirt and towel. When he had appeared at the magistrates' court after being charged the court had ordered an independent psychiatric report. This had recommended psychiatric treatment. However, the prison authorities insisted that he had to have a secure bed and this would only become available on 15 January. Paul Worrell killed himself three days before he was to be moved, four months after his arrest.

## Racism and Rastafarians

Among those who govern and run the prison system in Britain, black people are regarded as a control problem both directly by antagonising white prisoners and indirectly, simply by existing and behaving normally. All black prisoners are therefore suspect in the eyes of the prison authorities, but of particular concern is the growing number of people coming into prison who are Rastafarian.

A Home Office circular sent to prison governors in 1976 excluded Rastafarianism as a religious denomination and instructed governors to inform inmates on reception that this could not be accepted for registration. In addition, the Home Office permitted governors to cut the locks of Rasta prisoners saying that it had confirmed with an Ethiopian Orthodox Church priest in the UK that long hair was not a requirement of the religion. This reflected a restrictive view of Rastafarianism as many Rastas do not follow the Orthodox Church, but, a Home Office minister claimed, showed 'that the Home Office and the prison department have taken a sensitive and concerned approach'.[32] Just how sensitive and concerned was well illustrated by a number of cases involving Rastas in prison which occurred while the circular was in force.

Steve Thompson was sent to prison in February 1977 on a robbery charge which he consistently denied. He was in Gartree in 1979 when the riot occurred over the drugging of Michael Blake. He was told by officers that he had to have his hair cut. He refused because of his adherence to Rastafarianism and was held down and tranquilised. When he regained consciousness he found his locks had been shorn. His protests themselves were seen by prison medical staff as evidence of some psychiatric disorder. Thompson was then moved to Durham where, it is claimed, he was assaulted by prison officers and kept in the hospital unit for one week. He was then sent back to Gartree where he was drugged and kept in solitary confinement for several months. Finally, just five days before he was due to be released, Thompson was told he was being moved to Rampton Special Hospital where his release would be entirely at the discretion of the Home Secretary. Thompson claims he was never given any explanation for the move and was simply committed after two doctors diagnosed him as schizophrenic. One of these doctors subsequently said that, in reaching his diagnosis, he had been misled by Home Office reports of Thompson's violence. Thompson has always denied such allegations and neither the Home Office nor the prison authorities have since tried to substantiate them.

After a concerted campaign by Thompson's family and friends, supported by the Black Prisoners' Welfare Scheme, Thompson was released from Rampton in March 1981 and given an absolute discharge. No explanation was ever forthcoming.[33]

In the same year, a Rasta woman was being abused and forcibly drugged in Holloway Prison. Abbena Simba Tola was not allowed a wrap to cover her head or to keep her knees covered as she was required to do as a Rasta. Instead she improvised with a pillowslip. When this was taken from her she covered her head with a pair of paper knickers only to be refused further paper knickers or sanitary towels. She was then injected with Depixol, a long lasting tranquiliser which had been used experimentally for control purposes on prisoners at Albany on the Isle of Wight.[34]

Another young Rasta, Roland Jeffers, was rushed to hospital in 1981 from Lincoln Prison after refusing food which did not conform to the requirements of his religion. Perhaps the most tragic case was that of Richard 'Cartoon' Campbell, who died in Ashford Remand Centre in March 1980 at the age of 19. Campbell had been arrested early on 1 March after police had received reports of a young black man attempting to break into a sports shop in Brixton. He appeared at Camberwell Green Magistrates' Court on Monday, 3 March, charged with attempted burglary, and was remanded to Lewes Remand Centre. A week later he appeared in court again, when his allegation that he had been framed by the police and his use of Rastafarian language created doubts in the mind of the magistrate as to his mental state, and he was remanded to Ashford Remand Centre for medical and psychiatric reports. Campbell soon began to refuse food and was judged to be schizophrenic by the Remand Centre's psychiatrist. This diagnosis was confirmed by an external psychiatrist on account of Campbell's many references to 'Jah' (the Rasta word for God), his continued statements that he wanted to help the poor and starving in Africa and his 'socially inappropriate behaviour' which meant his lounging in a chair and looking out of the window while he was being examined. Two days later, Campbell was found collapsed in his cell and the next day he was transferred to a local mental hospital where he was examined by a psychiatrist yet again. This psychiatrist found him quite normal but was prepared to keep him in for observation. He was not prepared to have a prison officer remain with him all the time as this would upset the other patients. The prison authorities refused and Campbell was returned to Ashford Remand Centre. He was then force-fed daily until 31 March, the day he was due to appear again in court, when he was found dead in his cell. He had died from choking at some point in the night. At the subsequent inquest the jury, while returning a verdict of 'death by self-neglect', added a rider criticising the lack of adequate medical staff and facilities at Ashford Remand Centre.[35] He was the third person to die in Ashford Remand Centre between 1973 and 1980. All three were black.[36]

It was only after such tragedies as these, and after the patronising remarks of Lord Scarman that the true Rasta (presumably opposed to the fake Rasta) is deeply religious, essentially humble and sad, 'the Rastafarians, their faith and their aspirations deserve more understanding and sympathy than they get from the British people,' that the government decided to look at the question of Rastas again. At the time of writing, instructions had been given to detention centres that Rastafarians should be allowed to retain their dreadlocks while consideration was being given by the Home Office 'to the desirability of allowing for the recognition of minority customs and beliefs'.[37] Changed official attitudes towards Rastafarians, however welcome in that they may avoid some of the excesses resulting from the present view, do not mean an end to racism in prisons. The problem of racism extends far beyond the operation of the system as it affects one particular group.

**Immigration prisoners: a forgotten minority**

Discussions of black people in prisons tend to forget one particular group of prisoners, those who are held under the provisions of the immigration laws. Such prisoners have existed since the 1920s. Before then, people held for further enquiries before being allowed into Britain or those held after they had been refused entry were generally held on board the ship on which they had come and were detained until it, or another ship, sailed to take them away again. The practice of holding people in prison grew up as delays in removing people increased. At first, immigrant prisoners were held in police cells, until the police themselves protested that such cells were not suitable for holding people for more than a few days. The Home Office then began to authorise prisons for the detention of immigrants. This was scarcely an improvement. In 1922, the Chief Inspector of Aliens decided to find out for himself what conditions were like and visited prisons in Liverpool, Manchester, Edinburgh and Glasgow. What he saw appalled him. Immigrant prisoners, he complained, were in fact worse off than convicted prisoners. The former were locked up for most of the time, the latter could at least work in association with other prisoners. In addition, even though they had committed no offence, they were punished like all other prisoners by being forbidden to speak to other prisoners at any time, while conversation with prison officers was limited to the giving and receiving of official orders or questions. Finally, they were unable to smoke or chew tobacco. The Chief Inspector described the situation of immigrant prisoners as an affront to a society which prided itself on its decency and its civilisation. The

Home Office response to this indictment of prison conditions was to issue an instruction to prison governors saying that immigrant prisoners should be allowed to associate together and to smoke or chew tobacco 'to a reasonable extent'. (The parallel with the late 1970s is striking. Then, when severely criticised by an all-party committee of MPs over immigration detention facilities at Harmondsworth, the Home Office response was to promise to provide a new table-tennis table.)

More restrictive immigration laws have resulted in the detention of large numbers of people. In 1973 1521 people were taken into prison under the Immigration Act. The average daily population was 160. In 1977 the figure was 1396, but the average daily population had risen to 221, and the average time spent in custody was nearly two months. In 1980 a total of 1137 people were detained as immigration prisoners, while the average daily population was 192. The decrease in numbers since 1977 has been due largely to the vigorous campaigning of the Joint Council for the Welfare of Immigrants and not to any change of heart on the part of the Home Office or the government. On one particular day, 22 July 1980, 112 people were detained under the 1971 Act, 29 as alleged illegal entrants, 61 recommended for deportation by the courts and 24 being deported under the Home Office's own powers. These 112 people came from 34 different countries but the majority came from Nigeria, Turkey, India, Pakistan and Ghana. Immigration prisoners included those recommended for deportation by the courts; a large number of these will be detained even though they were not given a prison sentence. Thus, in 1980 the number of people detained in prison following a non-custodial sentence and a recommendation for deportation by the court was 222.

The conditions of immigration prisoners differ little from those of other prisoners. They are held in the same institutions, in the same cramped and unsanitary conditions, subject to the same restrictions on visits and contact with the outside world. Yet most have never been convicted of any offence. These conditions are not new and have existed ever since the practice of holding immigrant detainees in prison began. Occasionally, protests have drawn attention to their plight. For example, in 1971 50

deportees petitioned the government over conditions in Pentonville Prison, claiming they were locked up 3 to a cell, sometimes
for periods of 45 hours. The Home Office response to this was to
point out that deportees got half-an-hour's recreation on Satur-
days. The period of 45 hours was therefore an exaggeration![38]
Two years later a letter was smuggled out to the National Council
for Civil Liberties complaining of the 'abysmal' hygiene and
sanitation in Pentonville, that people who complained were punished and that medical services were sub-standard. The allegations were substantially supported by other letters and statements. Shortly afterwards three men barricaded themselves in
their cell in protest, and a few months later 39 immigrant prisoners
began a hunger strike in protest at the conditions. When the
protest ended, two men, a white South African and a German,
were disciplined for attempting to renew the protest and for
'inciting prisoners to commit acts of indiscipline'.[39]

In spite of such protests the government continues to imprison
people who have not committed any offence but who are treated
as though they have. Their situation is just one more consequence
of the operation of immigration controls whose function is not
simply to keep some people out of the country but to remove
some of those already here.

### The official response

Apart from giving prison staff some information about minority
religions, diet and dress, and issuing the 1976 circular on Rastafarians, it seems that the prison authorities took little interest in
the question of 'race' until the late 1970s and early 1980s. By
then, presumably, the danger of racial violence inside penal
institutions was sufficiently threatening that something had to be
done by the authorities. The spectre of the 1971 Attica prison
revolt in the United States, in which 43 prisoners and staff died
when the prison was stormed by the National Guard, figured
prominently in the minds of the prison authorities. It was no
coincidence that during the extended prison crisis of the late
1970s more than one governor warned of the possibility of an
Attica-type situation in Britain. The response of the prison

authorities was similar in many respects to what had been developed in policing.

The report of a seminar for governors held in 1980 concluded that racism was not generally perceived as a serious issue in prisons but through its 'all pervasive, unintended effects . . . the Prison Service has as great a problem as the other agencies of police and law enforcement'. On the face of it this is an astonishing statement. As we have seen, there is sufficient information to show the prevalence of racism within British prisons. What is more, we are entitled to assume that there is considerably more evidence available to the prison authorities, given that they run the institutions and control the flow of information from them. But if racism was not seen as a serious issue, what was the problem that presented itself to the prison service? Presumably it was the problem of the presence of black people – as indicated by some of the remarks made by prison staff. It is borne out by a statement made by Home Office minister Patrick Mayhew when he told MPs, 'One cannot deny that the presence of members of the ethnic minorities in our prisons occasionally poses problems. Staff must develop an understanding with all prisoners, not only as an aid to keeping control, but also as a means of exercising positive influence over them.'[40] The logic of these arguments about the presence of significant numbers being a problem is to implement a policy of dispersal. The classification of ethnic origins is a preliminary step in such a policy. Dispersal away from one's home area isolates the prisoner even more from family and friends, making it even more difficult for them to visit. More important, as with immigration control and its basis in the numbers game, such a policy not only avoids the question of racism but exacerbates it by focusing on black people as the problem.

The prison authorities also decided in 1981 to imitate the police in the appointment of race relations liaison officers, whose job it would be to assist, inform and enable other officers in their dealings with black people. Again, this avoids the issue: it poses the question entirely as one of making information available rather than in dealing with the attitudes, practices and structures through which racism is perpetuated. As with the police, it relegates the responsibility of the prison authorities to treat all equally to one officer, and thereby absolves other officers from their responsibility.

Finally, the prison authorities, again emulating the police, have indicated that attempts must be made to recruit more black prison officers. It is not known how many such officers there are but they are certainly few – not surprising if the treatment of the first black officer at Pentonville is anything to go by. This officer arrived at the prison when Tom Clayton was there researching his book *Men in Prison*. Clayton reported that the officers were critical of the new recruit. Had not the prison got enough social tensions without volunteering for another one, they asked. Others claimed that once there was one black officer, there would soon be 'enough to swamp the white officers'. Just to drive the point home, one letter to the officer from his wife was scrawled with the words 'Nigger' and 'Pig'.[41]

The prison service and penal institutions are therefore both a mirror of society and a microcosm of it, so far as black people and racism are concerned. Officially, it is black people who are the problem. Their numbers in any one place at one time have to be strictly controlled while racialism among staff is ignored or not admitted in public. Gestures are made towards acknowledging the existence of minorities but these are marginal and do not address the central question of structural racism. Meanwhile, the prison service relegates its responsibilities to specialist liaison officers.

The Director General of the prison service once spoke of an objective of the service being that of 'reflecting the spirit in which successive governments have made commitments to a multi-racial society'.[42] Given that the reality of the British 'multi-racial society' is that of structural racism, persistent and widespread discrimination, and increasing harassment by the forces of 'law and order', the prison service can be said to have achieved one of its two objectives.

# 7. Conclusion

The treatment of black people described in this book cannot be explained simply by the existence of racist individuals. They cannot be used to explain the depth and extent of racism, nor can they account for the failure of measures taken to deal with discrimination. We have to look at the context in which such individuals and organisations operate.[1]

Immigration law defined the presence of black people – not white racism – as the problem. Such an approach did not appease racists by making concessions. On the contrary, it provided fertile ground for racism to flourish. Government had defined black people as the problem and institutionalised racism in the law. Racists could take their lead from that.

The police, courts and prisons offered their own definition of the 'black problem'. Black people, it was argued, were a 'law and order' problem. At first this was couched primarily as black people's mistrust of the police, and community relations work was designed specifically to deal with this lack of trust. Increasingly this view gave way to one in which black people were seen as being openly disorderly, unruly and criminal. This process of criminalisation – of turning a section of the population into criminals – provided a justification for the abuse of black people because, for example, the police could show they needed to behave in an exceptional way because they were dealing with an exceptional problem. When challenged, as they were by the Scarman Report, all they had to do was provide 'proof' to the public by means of misleading statistics.

The white public was shown a black population extensively involved in criminal activity of one kind or another, facing serious charges and special procedures in the courts, disproportionately represented in the prison population, and presenting the prison system with serious problems as a result. To the white person in the street, 'black' increasingly meant crime and disorder. Criminalisation is not, however, an end in itself, nor is it simply a justification for harsher policing methods, tougher laws, or stricter prison regimes. It is a reflection and a very central expression of racism in Britain in a period of political crisis.

The crisis of the British state in the 1970s and 1980s is different from previous crises, not just in its depth and duration. It is of a qualitatively different order from previous crises. It has its roots, as Stuart Hall has said, in the structural backwardness of the British economy, combined with a change in Britain's position in the world economy and world politics.[2] It is a crisis of the political system itself, which is challenged on a scale unprecedented in modern times. These challenges to the authority and legitimacy of the system included, in the 1960s, the civil rights struggle of the Catholic minority in Northern Ireland, the direct action of the Campaign for Nuclear Disarmament, the anti-Vietnam war movement and, on the industrial front, a resurgence of rank-and-file militancy. These continued into the 1970s when the civil rights struggle in Northern Ireland gave way to an armed struggle.

On mainland Britain, it is in the black community that dissent and opposition have been most considerable. Black people have not been prepared to accept the inferior status increasingly forced on them. They have not been prepared to work the most unpleasant shifts at work for less money than white workers. They have not been prepared to have their children sent off to second-class schooling in units for the 'disruptive' or the educationally 'sub-normal'. They have not been prepared to submit passively to deportations of those living here or the division of families as a result of immigrations laws. They have not been prepared to submit to racist policing or to the racist violence against them which the police ignored.

Confrontation has been at a higher level in the black community for a number of reasons. First, immigration control not only defined black people as a problem for the state to black people as one of antagonism. A state that allocated considerable resources to keeping black people out of the country and to challenging the right of others to be here or to have access to benefits here, could not consistently pretend benevolence or even neutrality in any other sphere. Second, black people had brought to this country vigorous cultures of resistance, cultures forged in the context of direct imperialist repression and which have been developed to meet repression here. Most important in this respect was the *political* nature of such resistance. As Jenny Bourne wrote:

> If you have been bought and sold, and lynched and raped, and oppressed and exploited, just because of your race, it is not hard to make the connection between racism and exploitation. And it is the consciousness of that connection, whether among West Indians or Asians and however arrived at (through slave or peasant exploitation), that makes for political struggle across race lines. [3]

Third, there was a growing number of black youths, born and brought up in Britain, who were unable even to find the 'shit work' which had been forced on their parents and which, even if available, they were making clear they were not prepared to tolerate.

The British state was faced with several simultaneous challenges to its authority and legitimacy. Its primary response was direct control and regulation to discipline the recalcitrant sections of the population, those regarded as ungovernable in any other way. In Northern Ireland, the army was employed to impose 'order' on Catholic areas in what was to become a state of permanent emergency in which the army, police and courts were given virtually unlimited powers. In Britain itself, states of emergency were also used by the Heath government to deal with industrial struggle, the use of troops to break strikes became a frequent occurrence, and measures were taken to restrict the unions by the use of law under the 1971 Industrial Relations Act. In the courts, right to trial by jury was limited, vetting of jurors was introduced in secrecy, and overtly political trials were frequent. On the streets, policing became increasingly confrontational and quasi-military, not just at demonstrations and similar situations, but on an everyday level in working-class, particularly black working-class, areas. In short, the 1970s was a period of the increased use of the criminal law and its enforcement agencies – the police, courts and prisons – in all areas of social and political life.[4]

Increased direct repression can easily prove counter-productive, as governments have discovered. Emergency laws and powers in Northern Ireland, far from solving the crisis, have hardened resistance. What the state required, if such measures were to succeed, was a popular consensus and support for exceptional measures. In Britain, in the 1960s and 1970s, there was no better way to mould this consensus and establish such support than through the use of racist ideas.

The use of racism in a time of crisis had occurred before. Stuart Hall, quoting James Walvin's history of black people in Britain, has reminded us that at a time of famine and rapidly expanding population in the last decade of the sixteenth century, Queen Elizabeth issued a proclamation that there were 'of late divers blackamores brought into the realm, of which kind there are alreadie here too manie'. She ordered that 'those kind of people be sent forth of the land'.[5]

Nearly four centuries later in the late 1960s, Enoch Powell addressed himself to the social crisis through the medium of race. Although Powell's speeches of the time are normally considered to be only about race, they were in fact about the general crisis of the social order itself. As Stuart Hall points out, they were directed 'at the conspiracy of radical and alien forces threatening the society, at what Mr Powell himself called the "Enemy Within" '. This enemy was within society itself, nameless but everywhere:

> He is 'the Other', he is the stranger in the midst, he is the cuckoo in the nest, he is the excrement in the letterbox. 'He' is – the blacks.[6]

Powell was removed from the shadow cabinet for making his 'race' speeches but his theme was to persist as the crisis deepened.

By the late 1970s the issue of race had become ever present in discussions about unemployment, inner cities, social security, housing, education and, of course, crime. This presence is rarely explicit and it is precisely because it does not have to be made explicit that race can be used so successfully to 'explain' the crisis in all its manifestations. Race connects with what significant numbers of people already feel and think and the various characterisations of black people 'make sense' to large numbers of white people. They 'know', for example, that black people take white jobs; they 'know' that black children cause problems for white children in schools, either because they cannot speak English (Asians) or because they are unruly and disruptive (West Indians); they 'know' that black people abuse the social security and health system; and they most certainly 'know' that black people are involved in crime. In other words, such characterisations connect with the ingrained popular racism of British society which has its roots in British involvement in slavery and colonial exploitation. The point has been put well by novelist Salman Rushdie:

> If you want to understand British racism . . . It is impossible even to begin to grasp the nature of the beast unless you accept its historical roots; unless you see that 400 years of conquest and looting, centuries of being told that you are superior to the fuzzy-wuzzies and the wogs, leave their stain on you all; that such a stain seeps into every part of your culture, your language and your daily life; and that nothing much has been done to wash it out. If you want proof of the existence of this stain, you can look at the huge, undiminished appetite of white Britons for television series, films, plays and books full of nostalgia for the Great Pink Age . . . Think, too, about the ease with which the English language allows the terms of racial abuse to be coined: wog, frog, kraut, dago, spic, yid, coon, nigger, Argie. Can there be another language with so wide-ranging a vocabulary of racist denigration?[7]

This making of connections is most apparent in relation to crime. Race does not have to be mentioned any more in connection with particular crimes. A sort of widely understood code makes it clear just what is meant when people talk of 'inner cities', 'mugging', 'street crime', Brixton, Lambeth, Toxteth, Moss Side. All have become synonymous with and symbols for 'black crime'.

The connection made is between a popular conception of black people as criminal and a fear of crime which is popular only in the sense that it has been turned by the media into a 'popular' fear.

It is worth noting here that the conception of black people as criminal can take more than one form. In its crude variant it is simply a stereotype of innate criminality, as exemplified by Metropolitan Police Commissioner Newman's description of Jamaicans as 'constitutionally disorderly . . . it's in their make up'.[8] Another variant has gained ground. It suggests that criminality is spawned by deprivation; crime is seen as an expected, almost natural result of unemployment and poverty combined with pathological black cultures. This view is expressed in the Scarman Report, and in an increasing volume of academic sociology. Jock Young and John Lea, for example, the principal writers of this kind, have explained the kind of policing the black community has suffered simply as a response to rising levels of crime. Such crime arises from the 'relative deprivation' of British-born blacks, combined with a 'political marginalisation' which can find no outlet for grievance.[9] What is completely absent from such accounts is an explanation of how such 'political marginalisation' occurred (the mainstream political parties tried to keep people out of the country and kept them out of their membership too) and a recognition of the political richness and success of black cultures of resistance. More important is the absence of any recognition of police racism as a factor in the relationship of police and black people. In effect, the authors end up with the position that it is black people who are the problem, not racism.

Race, therefore, is the means by which the crisis is explained to the mass of the white public. In all areas of life, it is black people who are seen to cause problems: it is black people who *are* the problem. This portrayal and perception of black people as the problem has been assisted and spurred on by the development of what has come to be called the 'new racism'.[10] This new racism does not necessarily assert explicitly, as the old racism did, that white is superior to black. It asserts that there are differences, that these differences are natural, and that they can give rise to equally natural antagonisms. Enoch Powell articulated this in 1969 when he said:

An instinct to preserve an identity and defend a territory is one of the deepest and strongest implanted in mankind. I happen to believe that the instinct is good, and that its beneficial effects are not exhausted.[11]

By this time, Powell had been exiled to the margins of the Tory party, but in less than a decade his ideas had moved to the centre of Tory thinking. In 1976, for example, Tory MP Ivor Stanbrook in a debate on immigration said:

Let there be no beating about the bush. The average coloured immigrant has a different culture, a different religion and different language. This is what creates the problem. It is not just because of race.[12]

Two years later Alfred Sherman, a key Tory thinker and director of the Tory Centre for Policy Studies, argued that the 'imposition of mass immigration from backward alien cultures' was just one symptom of a 'self-destructive urge reflected in an assault on . . . all that is English and wholesome'.[13] Just how far such ideas had penetrated mainstream Tory thinking was shown by Margaret Thatcher when, only one year before she became Prime Minister, she told an interviewer that

people are really rather afraid that this country might be swamped by people with a different culture. And, you know, the British character has done so much for democracy, for law, and done so much throughout the world, that if there is a fear that it might be swamped, people are going to react and be rather hostile to those coming in.[14]

The fair-minded, benevolent British character which has done so much throughout the world cannot be blamed for its hostility to those who are different. Such antagonism is presented by the leaders of the Tory party as the most natural thing in the world. Flowing from this belief in natural differences, leading to natural antagonism, the new racism has also involved a resurgence and reworking of the idea of nation as the most important and most central expression of this 'natural' tendency of similar people to group together. The importance of the idea of the 'nation' was in the new racism as illustrated in the 1969 quotation from Enoch Powell referred to earlier. Powell was not alone in the importance he attached to the idea of nation; he was, in a sense, ahead of his time.

Only seven years later, Alfred Sherman in an article in the *Daily Telegraph* wrote of 'the assault . . . on all that is British and wholesome' and argued for a resolution of what he saw as the confusion between citizenship and nationhood. The former was a mere legal technicality, for although parliament could confer citizenship on whomever it wished it could 'no more turn a Chinese into an Englishman than it can turn a man into a woman.'[15] On the other hand nationhood was important because it was 'the natural cultural and historical heritage of true born Britons'. He pursued the theme the following day in a piece entitled 'Britain's urge to self-destruction'. Mass immigration, he argued, was a symptom of a self-destructive urge aimed at nationhood. In words which Margaret Thatcher would echo two years later, Sherman warned that while 'national consciousness like any other major human drive . . . is a constructive force provided legitimate channels; thwarted and frustrated it becomes explosive.'

Sherman returned in 1979 to the theme of nationhood on the occasion of the debate on immigration rule changes restricting the entry of foreign born husbands and fiances. In 'Britain is not Asia's fiance', Sherman maintained that the question of whether women should be permitted to bring in their foreign husbands or fiances was part of something much larger:

> The Asian fiances issue is the visible tip of a submerged but inescapable problem: the conflict between the instincts of the people and the intellectual fashions of the establishment where British nationhood is concerned.

National consciousness and national character were, he claimed,

> reflected in the way of life, political culture and political institutions no less than in culture. The difference between the social and political institutions in this country and those in the Indian sub-continent, the Caribbean or Africa – or for that

matter Russia or China – reflect this national character among other things.

Furthermore, Sherman wrote, in many cases

migrants bring with them anti-British attitudes. They are encouraged to take all benefits for granted and blame all short-comings on discrimination. They are also encouraged to see immigration restrictions as something to be circumvented.[16]

Other Tory thinkers were to make use of the same theme. Thus, at the time of the Falklands war, Peregrine Worsthorne noted the connection between war and the 'nation'. He wrote:

Although Britain is a multi-racial society, it is still very far from being a multi-racial nation. Its heart does not beat as one. Only in war does a nation discover what really 'turns it on'.[17]

What 'turned the nation on', Worsthorne had earlier said, was the protection of 'kith and kin', the 'heeding of ancestral voices summoning us to be true to the nation's past'.[18]

What is clear about the concept of nation in these and other accounts is that it refers to the concept of a white nation which, by its nature, excludes black people. They may be *in* Britain but they are not *of* it. Often the exclusion is explicit as it is, for example, in Sherman's distinction between citizenship and 'national identity'. The English, Scots, Welsh and Ulstermen have, he said, 'no other motherland. Its history, institutions, landmarks are an essential part of their personal identity. They wish to survive for future generations as an identifiable national identity . . . Their national identity is a birthright.' For the 'jet age migrants and their communities' on the other hand, 'Britain is simply a haven of convenience where they acquire rights without national obligations'.[19]

Worsthorne, too, has made explicit the excluding nature of British 'nationhood'. During the Falklands war he wrote, no doubt correctly, that 'if the Falkland Islanders were British citizens with black or brown skins . . . it is doubtful whether the Royal Navy and Marines would today be fighting for their liberation.'[20] Thatcher also made the point when she spoke in

1978 of an 'alien culture' and its threat of swamping. But even when she was not talking directly about race the exclusive idea of the 'nation' was evident in her post-Falklands 'victory speech' at Cheltenham:

> We have learned something about ourselves, a lesson which we desperately needed to learn. When we started out, there were the waverers and the fainthearts. The people who thought we could no longer do the great things which we once did . . . that we could never again be what we were. There were those who would not admit it . . . but – in their heart of hearts – they too had their secret fears that it was true: that Britain was no longer the nation that had built an Empire and ruled a quarter of the world. Well, they were wrong.[21]

As Salman Rushdie points out, Thatcher's use of the word 'we' was in itself excluding of black people in Britain. They did not feel the same about the Empire.

But this exclusion of black people from the 'nation' or the 'national culture' is made also at an everyday level. Thus, the long history of black people in Britain and their contribution to all areas of life is erased from the public memory. Attempts are made increasingly to emphasise how different black people are. They have, it is emphasised, their own languages, their own customs, their own dress, food, religions and, particularly important, their own connections with other countries. Black people, in other words, hold to values which are not British. This new racism therefore reasserts and reworks the idea of nation as something natural, while at the same time emphasising the otherness, the alienness of those regarded as different. Criminalisation of the black community takes this further and meshes race – the ideological response to the political crisis – with law and order – the authoritarian, practical response – in a way that is unique. The 'alien' population is thus presented to the public not just as alien, but as an explicit and overt threat to the 'nation'. This connection was made by Powell during the summer of 1981. In parliament he spoke of the 'ultimate reality, the ultimate cause, the *sine qua non*, without which what we have witnessed and are witnessing could not and would not have happened'. He continued:

Are we seriously saying that so long as there is poverty, unemployment and deprivation, our cities will be torn to pieces, that the police in them will be the objects of attack and that we shall destroy our environment? Of course not. Everyone knows that, although these conditions do exist, there is a factor which the people concerned perfectly well know, understand and apprehend, and which unless it can be dealt with – unless the fateful inevitability, the inexorable doubling and trebling, of that element of a population can be avoided – their worst fears will be fulfilled.[22]

There was no need for Powell to spell out what he was saying. Without mentioning race or black people, his message was clear. There would have been no riots or disorder, but for the presence of an 'alien' factor – the presence of black people.

The new racism is different from the old, not just in its component ideas. It is different also in its function. Racism is not the same for all times. It is specific to different periods and different contexts. During the period of slavery, racism served to justify the practice of buying and selling black people as though they were objects, not human beings. When slavery was abolished as it was no longer profitable, racism served to justify the conquest and exploitation of whole countries by European states. It justified the barbarism that accompanied such conquest and exploitation – murder, rape and pillage. A body of 'knowledge' was developed to 'prove' that people who were not white were inferior to whites, fit only to be ruled and to serve their white masters who might do with them as they pleased.

Eventually, the practice that followed from such ideas had to give way to the political reality of revolt by subjected populations and declining profitability of colonies which required ever more resources to keep them under control. Gradually, political independence was granted to the colonies, usually involving some form of continued economic dependence. One aspect of this new relationship was that ex-colonies became a source of cheap labour for the British economy.

Alongside this changed relationship, racism changed too. It came home, so to speak, to become domesticated. Even in this domestic variety, the function of racism was still the same: it justified exploitation. Black people came to Britain to do the jobs the white working class did not want. They were paid less, enjoyed fewer benefits and, of course, the cost of their upbringing had not been borne by the British state but by their native countries. It was, in other words, a bargain for capital. Sivanandan puts the point well:

> You discriminate in order to exploit or, which is the same thing, you exploit by discriminating . . . racism helped capital to make extra profit off black workers (extra in comparison to indigenous workers).[23]

Now the black population is no longer needed, even to be exploited. It has outlived its usefulness. It is a surplus population whose labour is no longer required and whose presence is no longer desired. There are, of course, other surplus populations, for example the growing numbers of the permanently unemployed. The black population is different because it can be regarded as an 'alien' surplus population, a population that does not belong here.

The logical place for a surplus population that is alien is therefore not Britain but elsewhere – 'home' – and the function of racism is no longer exploitation but repatriation. This repatriation is not of the enforced variety – that remains the daydream of the marginal fascist groups. It is repatriation by inducement and encouragement. The inducement may be financial and a growing body of opinion within the Tory party itself stands for substantial increases in existing repatriation allowances to encourage more people to 'go home'. But more important, the new repatriation comprehends 'all those measures whose effect is to make life untenable for black people in Britain'.[24]

Such measures of 'inducement' are now widespread. They include: the division of families by immigration officers who dispute that wives are genuinely married to husbands or children are genuinely the offspring of their parents; the ban on the entry of foreign husbands or fiances or, to put it another way, the enforced departure of wives and fiancees if they wish to live with their partners; increased resources and activities of the police and immigration service in searching for 'illegal' entrants; the widening by the courts and the Home Office of the definition of 'illegal entrant' and the resultant undermining of security of those settled here; and the increasing connection between immigration status and access to such rights as housing, health service treatment and social security which has led to more and more black people being questioned on the grounds that they may be excluded from access to such benefits. There is police harassment and the criminalisation of a whole community by the police. Racial violence exists on an unprecedented scale – a terror which, if not sanctioned by the police and the state, is allowed to continue by their inaction, backed up by the courts and the prisons. On all fronts the message to those on the receiving end is clear: if you want to live in peace, go home. The alternative, if such it can be called, is to accept a status which is second class.

The problem for the state is that black people are neither prepared to 'go home' – an increasing number know of no other home than Britain – or to accept any status inferior to that of the white population. This unwillingness has been shown on all fronts. In industry it has been shown in strikes such as those at Imperial Typewriters, Mansfield Hosiery, Chix and Grunwick; in education – anti-busing campaigns, struggles against the labelling of black pupils as educationally sub-normal or disruptive, and the provision of black schools to make up for the deficiencies of the state system; in immigration – demonstrations and lobbies against racist legislation and campaigns fought around individual cases, such as those of Anwar Ditta, Nasira Begum and the many other people divided from their families or threatened with deportation; in policing – the organisation of self-defence of the community against racist violence, confrontations with the police which reached their peak on the streets in the summer of 1981; in the courts – by means of defence campaigns based in the community; in prisons – by the solidarity of black prisoners in the face of prison brutality and racist brutality. In short, the black community's response to the message of 'go home' is that it is a community 'here to stay' and, if that stay is threatened, 'here to fight'.[25]

Such struggles of black people will continue, under their own control, with or without white support. It remains for white people generally, and the white left in particular, to grasp the importance of racism in the 1980s, to see that racism is the means by which the state responds to crisis and in doing so divides the working class against itself. It is increasingly the means by which authoritarian measures of state control can be made with popular support. Unless this is understood, reformist plans to make the police accountable to local authoities or to tackle racial discrimination by means of law, for example, will come to nothing. For, as Stuart Hall has reminded us, racism – and its answer – is not a matter of *policy* but of politics.[26] As the ideas of the new racism take firmer root, as the authoritarian response to the crisis increases in intensity, and as black people bear the brunt of this combination of ideology and practice, the urgency of understanding and combating British racism and its practical results is great indeed.

# Notes

## Preface

1. See for example: Centre for Contemporary Studies, *The Empire Strikes Back: Race and Racism in 70s Britain*, Hutchinson 1982, especially chapter 5; Gus John, *In the Service of Black Youth*, National Association of Youth Clubs 1981; and the *Bulletins* of the No Pass Laws Here group.
2. See A. Sivanandan, *Race and Resistance: The IRR Story*, Institute of Race Relations 1974; and Jenny Bourne, 'Cheerleaders and ombudsmen: the sociology of race relations in Britain', *Race & Class*, vol. XXI, no. 4, spring 1980, for an examination of some aspects of this.

## 1. State racism

1. Lord Scarman, *The Scarman Report*, Penguin 1982, para. 2.22.
2. Paul Foot, *Immigration and Race in British Politics*, Penguin 1965.
3. Cmnd. 2739, HMSO 1965.
4. Robert Moore, *Racism and Black Resistance in Britain*, Pluto Press 1975, p. 27.
5. *The Unpublished Report: the European Commission of Human Rights and British Immigration Policy*, Joint Council for the Welfare of Immigrants (JCWI) 1979.
6. Cited in Andrew Nicol, *Illegal Entrants*, JCWI/Runnymede Trust 1981, p. 38.
7. Paul Gordon, *Passport Raids and Checks: Britain's Internal Immigration Controls*, Runnymede Trust 1981, p. 74.
8. *ibid*. p. 65.
9. *Anti-Discrimination Legislation*, Political and Economic Planning (PEP) 1967.

10. A. Sivanandan, 'Race, class and the state: the black experience in Britain' in *A Different Hunger*, Pluto Press 1982, p. 117.
11. E. J. B. Rose et al, *Colour and Citizenship*, Oxford University Press/Institute of Race Relations 1969, p. 181.
12. Cmnd. 6234, HMSO 1975.
13. *The Extent of Racial Discrimination*, Political and Economic Planning (PEP) 1974.
14. *Race and Council Housing in London*, Runnymede Trust 1975.
15. Paul Gordon, *Incitement to Racial Hatred*, Runnymede Trust 1982.
16. *Commission for Racial Equality*, HC 46, HMSO 1982.
17. *The Scarman Report, op. cit.*, para. 8.49.
18. *op. cit.*, p. 120.
19. Ann Dummett, *A Portrait of English Racism*, Penguin 1973, p. 189.

## 2. Police against black people

1. Quoted in *CARF*, no. 9, 1979.
2. *New Statesman*, January 1981.
3. *Final Report of the Working Party on Community/Police Relations*, Lambeth Borough Council 1981.
4. Quoted in Lord Scarman, *The Scarman Report*, Penguin 1982, para. 4.39.
5. *Hansard*, 29 October 1981.
6. Quoted in Derek Humphry, *Police Power and Black People*, Panther 1972, p. 13.
7. Gus John, *Race in the Inner City*, Runnymede Trust 1970.
8. AFFOR, *Talking Blues*, 1978.
9. Campaign Against Racism and Fascism, *Southall: The Birth of a Black Community*, Institute of Race Relations 1982.
10. Sir Robert Mark, *In the Office of Constable*, Collins 1978, pp. 141–42.
11. Unofficial Committee of Enquiry, *The Death of Blair Peach*, NCCL 1981, p. 49.
12. *23 April 1979*, Southall Rights 1979.
13. *New Statesman*, 27 March 1981.
14. The *Guardian*, 19 March 1981.
15. *The Times*, 2 May 1981.
16. The *Guardian*, 8 June 1981.
17. *Caribbean Times*, 24 July 1981.
18. *Hansard*, 22 April 1982.

19. The *Daily Telegraph*, 24 April 1982.
20. *Police Against Black People*, Institute of Race Relations 1979.
21. Clare Demuth, *Sus: a Report on Section 4 of the Vagrancy Act 1824*, Runnymede Trust 1978.
22. ' "Sus" is dead. But what about "Sas"?', *New Community*, spring–summer 1981.
23. Merseyside Police Authority, *The Merseyside Disturbances: the Role and Responsibility of the Police Authority*, 1981.
24. *Black and Blue: Racism and the Police*, Communist Party 1981.
25. *Police and the Notting Hill Community*, North Kensington Law Centre 1982.
26. *Police Against Black People, op. cit.*, 1979.
27. *The Times*, 23 July 1970.
28. The *Daily Mirror*, 28 January 1981.
29. Philip Stevens and Carole Willis, *Race, Crime and Arrests*, Home Office 1979.
30. Maureen Cain and Susan Sadigh, *Journal of Law and Society*, vol. 9, no. 1, summer 1982.
31. This section is based on Paul Gordon, *Passport Raids and Checks: Britain's Internal Immigration Controls*, Runnymede Trust 1981.
32. *Police Against Black People, op. cit.*
33. Re-printed in *Race & Class*, vol. XXIV, no. 2, autumn 1982.
34. *Time Out*, 23 June 1979.
35. *City Limits*, 8 January 1982.
36. *New Statesman*, 15 January 1982.
37. *Police Against Black People, op. cit.*, p. 7.
38. The *Guardian*, 1 September 1976.
39. The *Guardian*, 12 August 1970.
40. The *Sun*, 3 March 1981.
41. 'Juveniles and the police', *British Journal of Criminology*, vol. 21, no. 1, January 1981.
42. *Race and Immigration*, no. 144, June 1982.
43. The *Guardian*, 8 August 1973.
44. The *Daily Mail*, 22 April 1980.
45. The *Guardian*, 9 June 1979.
46. The *Guardian*, 9 March 1981.
47. These cases were reported in *Searchlight*, March 1980.
48. The *Morning Star*, 29 August 1979.
49. The *Guardian*, 22 October 1981.
50. E. J. B. Rose et al, *Colour and Citizenship*, Oxford University Press/Institute of Race Relations 1969.

51. Derek Humphry, *Police Power and Black People*, Panther 1972.
52. The *Observer*, 24 January 1982.
53. *The Times Law Report*, 3 January 1983.
54. *Ethnic Minorities and Complaints Against the Police*, Home Office 1982.
55. Francesca Klug, *Racist Attacks*, Runnymede Trust 1982.
56. Simon Jenkins, *Here to Live: a Study of Race Relations in an English Town*, Runnymede Trust 1970.
57. The *Observer*, 5 April 1970.
58. *Race Today*, February 1971.
59. *The Sunday Times*, 18 March 1973.
60. Stanislaus Pullé, *Police/Immigrant Relations in Ealing*, Runnymede Trust 1973.
61. The *Guardian*, 3 May 1975.
62. *The Times*, 1 August 1975.
63. *The Times*, 22 June 1976.
64. *Hansard*, 31 October 1980.
65. *Racial Violence in Britain*, Joint Committee Against Racialism, 1981.
66. *Police Against Black People, op. cit.*
67. Francesca Klug, *Racist Attacks*, Runnymede Trust 1982.
68. *The Times*, 10 February 1981.
69. *Searchlight*, August 1982.
70. *The Voice*, 18 September 1982.
71. *Race and Immigration*, no. 149, November 1982.
72. These examples are taken from Francesca Klug, *op. cit.*
73. *CARF*, no. 7, 1978.
74. *Searchlight*, August 1982.
75. *Rights*, January–February 1979.

## 3. Police public relations

1. Superintendent Lawrence Roach, 'The Metropolitan Police Community Relations Branch', *Police Studies*, vol. 1, no. 3, September 1978.
2. *The Times*, 25 July 1977.
3. The *Guardian*, 14 January 1978.
4. Unofficial Committee of Enquiry, *Southall: 23 April 1979*, NCCL 1980.
5. *60 Days in the Indian Sub-continent*, City of Glasgow Police 1974.
6. *Race Today*, November 1970.
7. *The Times*, 18 May 1982.

8. *The Times*, 26 October 1982.
9. *Police Probationer Training in Race Relations*, Home Office 1982.
10. *Police Against Black People*, Institute of Race Relations 1979.
11. The *Guardian*, 9 December 1982.

## 4. Understanding police racism

1. Stuart Hall, *Drifting into a Law and Order Society*, Cobden Trust 1980.
2. Tony Judge, *A Man Apart*, Arthur Barker, 1972.
3. 'Conservatism, dogmatism and authoritarianism in British police officers', *Sociology*, January 1982.
4. *Policing London*, no. 4, November 1982.
5. 'Coloured immigrant communities and the police', *Police Journal*, April 1972.
6. The *Guardian*, 12 August 1971.
7. *The Sunday Times*, 5 January 1975.
8. The *Guardian*, 12 April 1976.
9. *The Sunday Telegraph*, 17 October 1976.
10. *The Scarman Report*, Penguin 1982, para. 1.4.
11. *ibid.*, para. 2.38.
12. *ibid.*, para. 4.56.
13. The *Daily Mail*, 11 March 1982.
14. *Searchlight*, April 1982.
15. Quoted in *The Times*, 25 March 1982.
16. *Police*, February 1982.
17. See *Race and Immigration*, no. 143, May 1982.
18. The *Guardian*, 15 March 1982. For a detailed account of this process see Joe Sim, 'Scarman: the police counter attack', *The Socialist Register*, 1982.
19. The *Guardian*, 25 September 1979.
20. *The Scarman Report, op. cit.*, para. 4.11.
21. The phrase is from A. Sivanandan, 'From resistance to rebellion' in *A Different Hunger*, Pluto Press 1982.

## 5. Racism and the courts

1. This section is based on Andrew Nicol, *Illegal Entrants*, JCWI/Runnymede Trust 1981.
2. Quoted in Nicol, *op. cit.*, p. 21.
3. The pre-1976 Act cases are discussed in J. A. G. Griffith, *The Politics of the Judiciary*, Fontana 1977.

4. Griffith, *op. cit.*, p. 201.
5. *ibid.*
6. *The Times*, 13 December 1979.
7. *The Times*, 28 February 1980.
8. *The Times*, 20 November 1981.
9. *The Times*, 5 October 1980.
10. *The Times*, 18 June 1982.
11. *The Times*, 30 July 1982.
12. *The Times*, 14 January 1978.
13. The *Guardian*, 2 February 1978.
14. *The Times*, 16 May 1975.
15. The *Daily Telegraph*, 10 April 1973.
16. *West Indian World*, 20 January 1978.
17. The *Guardian*, 25 January 1978.
18. The *Glasgow Herald*, 17 June 1981.
19. Personal communication.
20. *The Sunday Times*, 19 December 1971.
21. *Race Today*, October–November 1971, July 1972.
22. *Race Today*, December 1974, June, July and November 1975.
23. *Race Today*, December 1976.
24. Geoff Robertson, *Whose Conspiracy?*, NCCL 1974.
25. *Time Out*, 5 August 1977.
26. Lewisham Community Relations Council, *Conspiracy and Community: What the Lewisham 19 Affair Has Meant*, 1979.
27. *Searchlight*, December 1981.
28. *Journal of Law and Society*, vol. 9, no. 1, summer 1982.
29. *Police Against Black People*, Institute of Race Relations 1979.
30. Robin Lewis, *Real Trouble: A Study of Aspects of the Southall Trials*, Runnymede Trust 1980.
31. The *Daily Express*, 3 June 1981.
32. *Searchlight*, December 1981.
33. Richard Vogler, 'Magistrates and civil disorder', *LAG Bulletin*, November 1982.
34. *The Times*, 18 March 1969.
35. The *Daily Telegraph*, 5 June 1969.
36. *The Times*, 3 June 1981.
37. The *Morning Star*, 7 June 1976.
38. *The Times*, 3 June 1981.
39. *The Times*, 11 November 1981.
40. The *Morning Star*, 5 May 1982.
41. *Hansard*, 18 May 1981.

42. *Police Against Black People, op. cit.*, pp. 18–29.
43. *The Times Law Report*, 2 July 1982.
44. 'The influence of race on sentencing in England', *Criminal Law Review*, October 1982.
45. *LAG Bulletin*, November 1982.
46. *Ethnic Minorities in Borstal*, Home Office 1981.
47. *Labour Weekly*, 30 January 1981.
48. *Probation and After Care in a Multi Racial Society*, CRE 1981.
49. Bruce Carrington and David Henney, 'Young Rastafarians and the Probation Service', *Probation Journal*, December 1981.
50. *The Times*, 2 November 1981.
51. Louis Blom-Cooper in *The Guardian*, 15 September 1980.
52. *Race and Immigration*, Runnymede Trust Bulletin, no. 148, October 1982, figures to end of 1981.
53. Quoted in D. G. T. Williams: 'Suspended sentence at common law', *Public Law*, 1963.
54. *The Times*, 28 June 1982.
55. The *Daily Telegraph*, 3 February 1976.
56. *Runnymede Trust Bulletin*, no. 114, November 1979.

## 6. Prison racism

1. *Hansard,* 16 April 1981.
2. Quoted in the *Guardian*, 4 January 1982.
3. The *Guardian*, 9 October 1981.
4. PROP, *'Don't Mark His Face': Hull Prison Riot 1976*, PROP, no date.
5. J. E. Thomas and R. Pooley, *The Exploding Prison*, Junction Books 1980.
6. HC 199, HMSO 1982.
7. The parallel with education is striking. In the 1960s, the Minister for Education, Edward Boyle, promulgated what became known as 'Boyle's law' which said that schools should not be allowed to have more than 30 per cent immigrant pupils. The result was the busing of black children to schools miles from their homes. The policy of dispersal was finally abandoned in the mid-1970s when it was challenged as being discriminatory.
8. *New Society*, 26 March 1970.
9. *Searchlight*, no. 19, 1976.
10. *Searchlight*, no. 17, 1976.
11. The *Observer*, 21 November 1976.

12. The *Observer*, 14 November 1976.

13. *Hansard*, 23 December 1976.

14. *Searchlight*, no. 31, 1978.

15. Quoted in *Searchlight*, March 1980.

16. The *Guardian*, 28 September 1981.

17. *Searchlight*, April 1982.

18. *West Indian World*, 18 August 1977.

19. The *Guardian*, 5 January 1982.

20. Quoted in *Searchlight*, March 1980.

21. *Searchlight*, April 1982.

22. The *Guardian*, 14 November 1982.

23. The *Observer*, 10 November 1982.

24. *The Sunday Times*, 13 April 1969.

25. *Race Today*, January 1971.

26. The *Guardian*, 4 April 1974.

27. *Race Today*, June 1974.

28. The *Guardian*, 4, 5, 6 January 1982.

29. *Prison Service Journal*, July 1981.

30. *The Times*, 6 September 1982. The full text is published in the PROP *Prison Briefing*, no. 3, 1982.

31. The *Guardian*, 23 February 1974.

32. *Hansard*, 16 April 1981.

33. Geoff Coggan and Martin Walker, *Frightened for My Life: An Account of Deaths in British Prisons*, Fontana 1982, p. 204.

34. *Searchlight*, November 1981.

35. Coggan and Walker, *op. cit.*, chapter 6.

36. *Hansard*, 3 July 1980.

37. *Hansard*, 25 January 1982.

38. *The Sunday Times*, 11 April 1971.

39. The *Guardian*, 23, 25, 28 August 1973.

40. *Hansard*, 16 April 1981.

41. *New Society*, 26 March 1970.

42. *Report on the Work of the Prison Department 1981*, Cmnd. 8543, HMSO 1982.

## 7. Conclusion

1. In writing this final chapter I have borrowed freely from several sources, in particular: A. Sivanandan, *A Different Hunger*, Pluto Press 1982; A. Friend and A. Metcalfe, *Slump City*, Pluto Press 1981; Centre for Contemporary Cultural Studies, *The Empire*

*Strikes Back: Race and Racism in 70s Britain*, Hutchinson 1982; Martin Barker, *The New Racism*, Junction Books 1981; and Stuart Hall *et al*, *Policing the Crisis*, Macmillan 1978.

2. 'Racism and Reaction' in *Five Views of Multi-Racial Britain*, CRE 1978.

3. 'Cheerleaders and ombudsmen: the sociology of race relations in Britain' in *Race & Class*, vol. XXI, no. 4, spring 1980, p. 345.

4. For a detailed account of this period see Stuart Hall *et al*, *Policing the Crisis*, Macmillan 1978, chapters 8 and 9.

5. 'Racism and Reaction', *op. cit.*, p. 23.

6. *ibid.*, p. 30.

7. Salman Rushdie, 'The new empire within Britain', *New Society*, 9 December 1982.

8. *Police Magazine*, (United States) January 1982.

9. 'Urban violence and political marginalisation: the riots in Britain, summer 1981' in *Critical Social Policy*, vol. 1, no. 3, spring 1982. For a critique of this position see Paul Gilroy, 'The myth of black criminality' in *Socialist Register 1982*, Merlin Press 1982.

10. The expression is Martin Barker's and the title of his lucid account of modern racism, Junction Books 1981.

11. Quoted in Barker, *op. cit.*, p. 15.

12. *Hansard*, 5 July 1976, quoted in Barker, *op. cit.*, p. 75.

13. The *Daily Telegraph*, 9 September 1976.

14. Quoted in *The Daily Mail*, 31 January 1978.

15. The *Daily Telegraph*, 8 September 1976.

16. The *Daily Telegraph*, 19 November 1979.

17. The *Sunday Telegraph*, 27 June 1982.

18. The *Sunday Telegraph*, 23 May 1982.

19. The *Daily Telegraph*, 9 November 1979.

20. The *Daily Telegraph*, 23 May 1982.

21. Quoted in Rushdie, *op. cit.*

22. *Hansard*, 18 July 1981.

23. 'Race, class and the state' in *A Different Hunger*, Pluto Press 1982, p. 113.

24. *Race & Class*, vol. XXIII, no. 2/3, autumn/winter 1982, p. 242.

25. For a wide-ranging and lucid account of black people's struggles of resistance see A. Sivanandan, 'From resistance to rebellion' in *A Different Hunger*, Pluto Press 1982.

26. 'Racism and reaction', *op. cit.*, p. 24.